Collins

PRACTICE MULTIPLE CHOICE QUESTIONS

CSEC®
Maths

T0318023

**Terry
David**

Collins

HarperCollins Publishers Ltd
The News Building
1 London Bridge Street
London SE1 9GF

First edition 2016

10 9 8 7 6 5 4 3 2

© HarperCollins *Publishers* Limited 2016

ISBN 978-0-00-819473-4

www.collins.co.uk/caribbeanschools

A catalogue record for this book is available from the British Library.

Typeset by QBS Learning
Printed and bound by Grafica Veneta S. P. A.

Author: Terry David
Publisher: Elaine Higgleton
Commissioning Editor: Ben Gardiner
Managing Editor: Sarah Thomas
Project Manager: Alissa McWhinnie
Copy Editor: Julie Gorman
Proofreader: Helen Bleck
Answer Checker: Rich Cutler
Artwork: QBS Learning
Cover design: Kevin Robbins and Gordon MacGilp
Production: Lauren Crisp

Contents

Contents (cont.)

Contents (cont.)

Download answers for free at www.collins.co.uk/caribbeanschools

Introduction

Structure of the CSEC Mathematics Paper 1 Examination

There are **60 questions**, known as items, in the Paper 1 examination and the duration of the examination is $1\frac{1}{2}$ **hours**. The paper is worth **30%** of your final examination mark.

The Paper 1 examination tests the following core areas of the syllabus.

Sections	*Approximate* Number of Questions
Computation	6
Number Theory	4
Consumer Arithmetic	8
Sets	4
Measurement	8
Statistics	6
Algebra	9
Relations, Functions and Graphs	6
Geometry and Trigonometry, and Vectors and Matrices	9
Total	**60**

The questions test two profiles, **knowledge and comprehension**, and **use of knowledge**. Questions will be presented in a variety of ways including the use of diagrams, data, graphs, prose or other stimulus material.

Each question is allocated 1 mark. You will <u>not</u> lose a mark if a question is answered incorrectly.

Examination Tips

General strategies for answering multiple choice questions

- Read every word of each question very carefully and make sure you understand exactly what it is asking. Even if you think that the question appears simple or straight forward there may be important information you could easily omit, especially small, but very important words such as *all* or *only*.

- When faced with a question that seems unfamiliar, re-read it very carefully. Underline or circle the key pieces of information provided. Re-read it again if necessary to make sure you are very clear as to what it is asking and that you are not misinterpreting it.

- Each question has four options, **A**, **B**, **C** and **D**, and only one is the correct answer. Look at all the options very carefully as the differences between them may be very subtle; never stop when you come across an option you think is the one required. Cross out options that you know are incorrect for certain. There may be two options that appear very similar; identify the difference between the two so you can select the correct answer.

- You have approximately $1\frac{1}{2}$ minutes per question. Some questions can be answered in less than 1 minute while other questions may require longer because of the reasoning or calculation involved. Do not spend too long on any one question.

- If a question appears difficult place a mark, such as an asterisk, on your answer sheet alongside the question number and return to it when you have finished answering all the other questions. Remember to carefully remove the asterisk, or other markings, from the answer sheet using a good clean eraser as soon as you have completed the question.

- Answer every question. Marks are not deducted for incorrect answers. Therefore, it is in your best interest to make an educated guess in instances where you do not know the answer. Never leave a question unanswered.

- Always ensure that you are shading the correct question number on your answer sheet. It is very easy to make a mistake, especially if you plan on returning to skipped questions.

- Some questions may ask which of the options is NOT correct or is INCORRECT. Pay close attention to this because it is easy to fail to see the words *NOT* or *INCORRECT* and answer the question incorrectly.

- Some questions may give two or more answers that could be correct and you are asked to determine which is the *BEST* or *MOST LIKELY*. You must consider each answer very carefully before making your choice because the differences between them may be very subtle.

- When a question gives three or four answers numbered **I**, **II** and **III** or **I**, **II**, **III** and **IV**, one or more of these answers may be correct. You will then be given four combinations as options, for example:

    A I only

    B I and II only

C I and III only

D I, II and III

Place a tick by all the answers that you think are correct before you decide on the final correct combination.

- Do not make any assumptions about your choice of options, just because two answers in succession have been C, it does not mean that the next one cannot be C as well.

- Try to leave time at the end of the examination to check over your answers, but never change an answer until you have thought about it again very carefully.

Strategies for the CSEC Mathematics Paper 1

- Calculators and mathematical tables are not allowed in this examination. Therefore you should be very careful and accurate when performing calculations. It is very easy to make an error and there may be an incorrect option similar to your calculation. You are allowed to write on the examination paper in order to perform calculations. Write as neatly as you can to avoid unnecessary errors.

- Even though calculators are not allowed, all the calculations in the Paper 1 examination can be done on paper. If a calculation is too challenging CXC will provide answers that show the intermediate steps rather than the final answer. In this way you do not have to worry about long arithmetic procedures that can be challenging under exam conditions.

- You should create a quick revision sheet a few weeks before the examination. There are some topics that require the use of formulas that are not provided in the paper. This is especially so for measurement questions. When revising for the Paper 1, draw the basic shapes like a square, triangle, rectangle, circle and trapezium on a sheet of paper. Write down the formula to determine the area and perimeter of these shapes.

  Draw a cube, cuboid, right pyramid, cone, cylinder and a sphere and write down the formula to find the volume of each. This can be used as a quick revision guide several days before the examination. Feel free to create quick revision sheets for other topics that give you some difficulty.

- When a diagram is provided for a particular question, make use of it. As you read the question insert all the information being provided. Insert information that can also be deduced. A diagram greatly improves your understanding of the question being asked. If one is not provided, draw one to help you answer the question.

Computation

Expressing a number in standard form

1 0.002 51 written in standard form is

   A 2.51×10^{3} Ⓐ

   B 2.51×10^{2} Ⓑ

   C 2.51×10^{-2} Ⓒ

   D 2.51×10^{-3} Ⓓ

2 0.0053 written in standard form is

   A 5.3×10^{-2} Ⓐ

   B 5.3×10^{-3} Ⓑ

   C 5.3×10^{3} Ⓒ

   D 5.3×10^{2} Ⓓ

Performing calculations involving decimals

3 Express 0.375 as a fraction in its lowest terms.

   A $\dfrac{1}{7}$ Ⓐ

   B $\dfrac{3}{8}$ Ⓑ

   C $\dfrac{5}{7}$ Ⓒ

   D $\dfrac{3}{7}$ Ⓓ

4 The exact value of $8 \div 0.002$ is

   A 4   Ⓐ

   B 40   Ⓑ

   C 400   Ⓒ

   D 4000   Ⓓ

5 $0.375 \times 0.03 =$

   A 0.001 125   (A)

   B 0.011 25   (B)

   C 1.125   (C)

   D 0.112 5   (D)

6 The exact value of $4 \div (0.1)^2$ is

   A 400   (A)

   B 4000   (B)

   C 0.04   (C)

   D 0.004   (D)

7 If $5.6 \times 0.52 = 2.912$, then $0.56 \times 520 =$

   A 0.002 912   (A)

   B 2.912   (B)

   C 29.12   (C)

   D 291.2   (D)

8 17.95×0.5 is approximately

   A 0.09   (A)

   B 0.9   (B)

   C 9   (C)

   D 90   (D)

9 The exact value of $(2.4 \times 1.2) + 3.6 =$

    A 6.48   Ⓐ

    B 64.8   Ⓑ

    C 0.648   Ⓒ

    D 0.0648   Ⓓ

10 The exact value of $\dfrac{19.5 \div 1.5}{1000}$ is

    A 0.013   Ⓐ

    B 0.13   Ⓑ

    C 1.3   Ⓒ

    D 0.0013   Ⓓ

11 The exact value of $(0.1)^2 + 4.21$ is

    A 4.22   Ⓐ

    B 4.212   Ⓑ

    C 4.2102   Ⓒ

    D 4.23   Ⓓ

Performing calculations involving fractions

12 $2\dfrac{2}{3} + 3\dfrac{1}{4} =$

    A $5\dfrac{3}{7}$ Ⓐ

    B $5\dfrac{3}{12}$ Ⓑ

    C $5\dfrac{11}{12}$ Ⓒ

    D $5\dfrac{7}{12}$ Ⓓ

13 $4\frac{3}{5} - 2\frac{1}{2} =$

   A $2\frac{2}{3}$ Ⓐ

   B $2\frac{1}{5}$ Ⓑ

   C $2\frac{2}{10}$ Ⓒ

   D $2\frac{1}{10}$ Ⓓ

14 What number when added to $3\frac{2}{5}$ gives 5?

   A $2\frac{1}{5}$ Ⓐ

   B $1\frac{2}{5}$ Ⓑ

   C $2\frac{3}{5}$ Ⓒ

   D $1\frac{3}{5}$ Ⓓ

15 $3\frac{2}{5} - 1\frac{1}{4} =$

   A $2\frac{1}{20}$ Ⓐ

   B $2\frac{5}{20}$ Ⓑ

   C $2\frac{3}{20}$ Ⓒ

   D $2\frac{7}{20}$ Ⓓ

16 $\left(\dfrac{3}{5} \times \dfrac{25}{24}\right) \div \dfrac{2}{3} =$

    A $\dfrac{5}{12}$ Ⓐ

    B $\dfrac{16}{15}$ Ⓓ

    C $\dfrac{13}{16}$ Ⓒ

    D $\dfrac{15}{16}$ Ⓓ

Expressing a number to decimal places and significant figures

17 The number 5.230 61 written correct to 3 decimal places is

    A 5.230   Ⓐ

    B 5.231   Ⓑ

    C 5.229   Ⓒ

    D 5.236   Ⓓ

18 Express $3\dfrac{5}{8}$ as a decimal correct to 3 significant figures.

    A 3.63   Ⓐ

    B 3.62   Ⓑ

    C 3.61   Ⓒ

    D 3.65   Ⓓ

19 0.002 347 written to two significant figures is

    A 0.002 3   Ⓐ

    B 0.002 4   Ⓑ

    C 0.002   Ⓒ

    D 0.002 35   Ⓓ

Performing a calculation using ratios

20 Anya, Daniel and Victoria shared some tokens for games in an arcade in the ratio 3:5:7. Daniel and Victoria together received a combined total of 36 tokens. What is the total number of tokens originally shared among the friends?

A 28   Ⓐ

B 15   Ⓑ

C 45   Ⓒ

D 60   Ⓓ

21 $120 is shared in the ratio 2:3. What is the larger share?

A $48   Ⓐ

B $72   Ⓑ

C $80   Ⓒ

D $60   Ⓓ

22 Yashoda and Ingrid shared a sum of money in the ratio 3:2, respectively. Ingrid received $1200. What was Yashoda's share?

A $800   Ⓐ

B $2000   Ⓑ

C $1500   Ⓒ

D $1800   Ⓓ

Performing a calculation involving percentages

23 What percentage of 40 is 5?

A 12.5%   Ⓐ

B 112%   Ⓑ

C 8%   Ⓒ

D 200%   Ⓓ

24 If 40% of a number is 120, what is the number?

A 48   Ⓐ

B 300   Ⓑ

C 72   Ⓒ

D 200   Ⓓ

25 $12\frac{1}{2}$ % of 800 is

A 100   Ⓐ

B 200   Ⓑ

C 400   Ⓒ

D 600   Ⓓ

26 What percentage of 270 is 90?

A 66.7%   Ⓐ

B 33.3%   Ⓑ

C 300%   Ⓒ

D 20%   Ⓓ

27 60% of a number is 120. What is the number?

A 48   Ⓐ

B 72   Ⓑ

C 100   Ⓒ

D 200   Ⓓ

28 A quiz is marked out of 60. Sandra gets 90%. What score did she get?

A 58   Ⓐ

B 40   Ⓑ

C 54   Ⓒ

D 50   Ⓓ

29 20% of a number is 30. What is 60% of the number?

A 30   Ⓐ

B 60   Ⓑ

C 90   Ⓒ

D 120   Ⓓ

30 60% of 1200 =

A 300   Ⓐ

B 720   Ⓑ

C 480   Ⓒ

D 600   Ⓓ

Estimating the square root of a number

31 If $16^2 = 256$, then $\sqrt{0.0256} =$

A 0.016   Ⓐ

B 0.16   Ⓑ

C 1.6   Ⓒ

D 0.0016   Ⓓ

32 $\sqrt{220}$ is approximately

A 1.5×10 Ⓐ

B 1.5×10^2 Ⓑ

C 2.2×10 Ⓒ

D 2.2×10^2 Ⓓ

33 The square root of 158 lies between

A 10 and 11   (A)

B 12 and 13   (B)

C 13 and 14   (C)

D 9 and 10   (D)

Performing exchange rate calculations

34 The exchange rate for 1 US dollar (US$1.00) is 6.50 TT dollars (TT$6.50).

What is the value of US$300 in TT currency?

A $1950   (A)

B $46.15   (B)

C $1250   (C)

D $27.25   (D)

Converting between units

35 How many centimetres are there in 2.5 metres?

A 25   (A)

B 0.25   (B)

C 0.025   (C)

D 250   (D)

36 3500 millimetres expressed in metres is

A 3.5   (A)

B 0.35   (B)

C 3 500 000   (C)

D 350   (D)

37 How many kilograms are there in 2.2 tonnes?

    A 22 kg   Ⓐ

    B 220 kg   Ⓑ

    C 2200 kg   Ⓒ

    D 22 000 kg   Ⓓ

Performing calculations involving indices

38 $(-2)^3 + (-1)^3 =$

    A -9 Ⓐ

    B -7 Ⓑ

    C 7 Ⓒ

    D 9 Ⓓ

39 $-\left(\dfrac{1}{3}\right)^3 =$

    A $-\dfrac{1}{9}$ Ⓐ

    B $-\dfrac{1}{27}$ Ⓑ

    C $\dfrac{1}{27}$ Ⓒ

    D $\dfrac{1}{9}$ Ⓓ

40 $(-3)^2 + (-1)^3 =$

    A 8 Ⓐ

    B 10 Ⓑ

    C -10 Ⓒ

    D 4 Ⓓ

2   Number Theory

Determining the highest common factor

1 The highest common factor of the set of numbers {36, 60, 96} is

  A 6   Ⓐ

  B 18   Ⓑ

  C 12   Ⓒ

  D 9   Ⓓ

2 Arrange the following fractions in ascending order of magnitude: $\frac{1}{2}, \frac{5}{6}, \frac{3}{4}, \frac{1}{12}$.

  A $\frac{1}{12}, \frac{1}{2}, \frac{3}{4}, \frac{5}{6}$ Ⓐ

  B $\frac{5}{6}, \frac{3}{4}, \frac{1}{2}, \frac{1}{12}$ Ⓑ

  C $\frac{1}{2}, \frac{3}{4}, \frac{5}{6}, \frac{1}{12}$ Ⓒ

  D $\frac{3}{4}, \frac{1}{2}, \frac{1}{12}, \frac{5}{6}$ Ⓓ

Determining the lowest common factor

3 What is the least number of marbles that can be shared equally among 2, 4 or 7 children?

  A 14   Ⓐ

  B 28   Ⓑ

  C 56   Ⓒ

  D 21   Ⓓ

4 The lowest common multiple of the set of numbers {6, 9, 12} is

  A 12   Ⓐ

  B 54   Ⓑ

  C 24   Ⓒ

  D 36   Ⓓ

5 The first three common multiples of 2, 3 and 4 are

   A 12, 24 and 36   Ⓐ

   B 1, 2 and 4   Ⓑ

   C 18, 24 and 32   Ⓒ

   D 16, 24 and 36   Ⓓ

Applying the distributive law

6 By the distributive law, $63 \times 18 + 63 \times 2 =$

   A 63×20 Ⓐ

   B $63 + 20$ Ⓑ

   C 65×81 Ⓒ

   D $65 + 81$ Ⓓ

Applying the associative law

7 $\left(\dfrac{1}{3} + \dfrac{1}{8}\right) + \dfrac{3}{5} = \dfrac{1}{3} + \left(\dfrac{1}{8} + \dfrac{3}{5}\right)$ illustrates which of the following properties?

   A Commutative property   Ⓐ

   B Distributive property   Ⓑ

   C Identity property   Ⓒ

   D Associative property   Ⓓ

Recognising prime numbers

8 The largest prime number that is less than 50 is

   A 45   Ⓐ

   B 46   Ⓑ

   C 47   Ⓒ

   D 49   Ⓓ

9 Which of the following numbers is prime?

   A 258   Ⓐ

   B 256   Ⓑ

   C 263   Ⓒ

   D 396   Ⓓ

Recognising odd and even numbers

10 If x is an even number, which of the following is necessarily even?

   A $x + 1$ Ⓐ

   B $x - 3$ Ⓑ

   C $2x - 1$ Ⓒ

   D $2x + 2$ Ⓓ

Recognising natural numbers

11 Which of the following represents the set of natural numbers?

   A $\{0, 1, 2, 3, \ldots\}$ Ⓐ

   B $\{1, 2, 3, \ldots\}$ Ⓑ

   C $\{\ldots, -2, -1, 0, 1, 2, \ldots\}$ Ⓒ

   D $\left\{\dfrac{1}{2}, \dfrac{3}{4}, \dfrac{7}{8}, \ldots\right\}$ Ⓓ

12 Which of the following numbers is rational?

   A $\dfrac{2}{\sqrt{5}}$ Ⓐ

   B $\sqrt{\dfrac{25}{36}}$ Ⓑ

   C $\dfrac{\pi}{2}$ Ⓒ

   D $\sqrt{31}$ Ⓓ

Recognising the next term in a sequence

13 The next term in the sequence 1, 1, 2, 3, 5, … is

   A 6   (A)

   B 7   (B)

   C 8   (C)

   D 9   (D)

14 The next term in the sequence 4, 7, 11, 16, … is

   A 22   (A)

   B 18   (B)

   C 32   (C)

   D 24   (D)

Determining place values

15 What is the value of the digit 3 in the number 25.634?

   A 3   (A)

   B 300   (B)

   C $\dfrac{3}{10}$ (C)

   D $\dfrac{3}{100}$ (D)

16 37×225 can be written as

   A $(37 \times 200) + (37 \times 25)$ (A)

   B $(37 \times 200) + 25$ (B)

   C $(37 + 200) \times (37 + 25)$ (C)

   D $(200 \times 37) + (200 \times 25)$ (D)

17 What is the place value of the digit 6 in the number 5642?

A 60

B 0.006

C 600

D 6

Ⓐ

Ⓑ

Ⓒ

Ⓓ

18 The number 365 can be written as

A $3 \times 10^3 + 6 \times 10^2 + 5 \times 10$

B $3 \times 10^3 + 6 \times 10^2 + 5$

C $3 \times 10^2 + 6 \times 10 + 5 \times 10^0$

D $3 \times 10^3 + 6 \times 10^1 + 5 \times 10^0$

Ⓐ

Ⓑ

Ⓒ

Ⓓ

3 Consumer Arithmetic

Determining simple interest

1 The simple interest earned on $1000 at 4% per annum for 5 years is

A $\dfrac{1000 \times 5}{4 \times 100}$

B $\dfrac{1000 \times 4 \times 5}{100}$

C $\dfrac{1000 \times 100}{4 \times 5}$

D $\dfrac{1000 \times 0.04 \times 5}{100}$

Ⓐ

Ⓑ

Ⓒ

Ⓓ

2 Jesse takes a loan for $10 000. The loan is paid back in 2 years by making monthly payments of $500. What was the annual interest rate of this loan?

A 10%　　　　　　　　　　　　　　　　　　　　　　　　　Ⓐ

B 15%　　　　　　　　　　　　　　　　　　　　　　　　　Ⓑ

C 20%　　　　　　　　　　　　　　　　　　　　　　　　　Ⓒ

D $12\frac{1}{2}$%　　　　　　　　　　　　　　　　　　　　　Ⓓ

3 $1200 invested at simple interest for 2 years earns $300. What is the rate of interest per annum?

A 5%　　　　　　　　　　　　　　　　　　　　　　　　　Ⓐ

B $12\frac{1}{2}$%　　　　　　　　　　　　　　　　　　　　　Ⓑ

C 10%　　　　　　　　　　　　　　　　　　　　　　　　　Ⓒ

D $2\frac{1}{2}$%　　　　　　　　　　　　　　　　　　　　　Ⓓ

4 Adam invested $300 for 4 years at 5% simple interest per annum. Ann invested $400 at the same rate. If they both received the same amount of money in interest, for how many years did Ann invest her money?

A 1　　　　　　　　　　　　　　　　　　　　　　　　　　Ⓐ

B 2　　　　　　　　　　　　　　　　　　　　　　　　　　Ⓑ

C 3　　　　　　　　　　　　　　　　　　　　　　　　　　Ⓒ

D 4　　　　　　　　　　　　　　　　　　　　　　　　　　Ⓓ

5 The simple interest on a loan of $12 000 for 4 years was $ 2400. What is the rate of interest per annum?

A 5%　　　　　　　　　　　　　　　　　　　　　　　　　Ⓐ

B 10%　　　　　　　　　　　　　　　　　　　　　　　　　Ⓑ

C 12%　　　　　　　　　　　　　　　　　　　　　　　　　Ⓒ

D 25%　　　　　　　　　　　　　　　　　　　　　　　　　Ⓓ

Performing hire purchase calculations

6 A flat-screen television cost $2000 cash. If the television is bought on hire purchase, a consumer must make a deposit of $900, followed by 12 monthly payments of $120. How much can be saved if the television is bought at the cash price?

A $780   (A)

B $300   (B)

C $340   (C)

D $100   (D)

Calculating taxes

7 A plot of land in Trinidad is valued at $250 000. Eddy wants to purchase the land. If the land is taxed at a rate of $0.80 per $100, what is the amount of tax Eddy would have to pay?

A $2000   (A)

B $800   (B)

C $200   (C)

D $1200   (D)

8 Andy's annual income is $60 000. His tax-free allowance is $15 000. His taxable income is taxed at a rate of 25%. The tax payable is

A $45 000   (A)

B $11 250   (B)

C $15 000   (C)

D $3750   (D)

9 Alex bought a T-shirt online for $150. As it was an online purchase he was taxed at a rate of 10%. He pays the delivery man $200. How much change does he get?

A $15   Ⓐ

B $165   Ⓑ

C $35   Ⓒ

D $20   Ⓓ

Calculating discounts and mark-ups

10 During a Christmas sale, a discount of 10% was being given on the marked price of all laptops. If the marked price of the laptop was $3000, what was the sale price?

A $3000   Ⓐ

B $2500   Ⓑ

C $2700   Ⓒ

D $300   Ⓓ

11 A tool in a local hardware store has an original price of $800. The price is increased by 12.5%. The new price of the tool is

A $900   Ⓐ

B $100   Ⓑ

C $1000   Ⓒ

D $800   Ⓓ

12 Jodi saved $120 when he purchased a small appliance at a sale. He received a discount of 15% on the marked price. What was the marked price of the appliance?

A $800   Ⓐ

B $18   Ⓑ

C $200   Ⓒ

D $600   Ⓓ

13 David Enterprises currently has a sales promotion. When a customer spends more than $1000 they receive a 5% discount on their purchase. Jade purchases items worth $1400. How much did she eventually pay at the cash desk?

A $70   (A)

B $400   (B)

C $1200   (C)

D $1330   (D)

Calculating insurance rates

14 Hope Insurance has a promotion for new homeowners. Their yearly rates are as follows:

Insurance rate for a home: 20 cents per $100.

Insurance rate for the contents of a home (furniture, appliances, etc.): 60 cents per $100.

Luke recently built a house. A valuator values his house at $600 000 and the contents at $100 000. How much insurance would Luke pay for the year?

A $1200   (A)

B $600   (B)

C $1800   (C)

D $5600   (D)

Calculating depreciation rates

15 Steve purchases a car for $180 000. The car depreciates at a rate of 10% per annum. What is the value of the car after <u>two</u> years?

A $162 000   (A)

B $145 800   (B)

C $160 000   (C)

D $150 000   (D)

16 A car purchased on January 1st has a value of $x. On December 31st the value of the car is $(0.95x). What is the rate of depreciation?

A 95% per year   Ⓐ

B 10% per year   Ⓑ

C 5% per year   Ⓒ

D 0.95% per year   Ⓓ

Calculating electricity rates

17 Electricity rates in a particular region are as follows:

Fixed meter rental	$3 per month
First 200 units	12 cents per unit
Usage in excess of 200 units	9 cents per unit

Adam receives an electricity bill for $54 in the month of June. How many units of electricity was he billed for?

A 300   Ⓐ

B 400   Ⓑ

C 500   Ⓒ

D 600   Ⓓ

Calculating profit and loss

18 Barry bought a smart phone for $2000. He eventually sold it for $2400. His profit as a percentage of his cost price is

A 10%   Ⓐ

B 15%   Ⓑ

C 20%   Ⓒ

D 25%   Ⓓ

19 A loan of $10 000 was paid back in 3 years in monthly instalments of $300. The percentage profit on the loan was

A 2%   (A)

B 4%   (B)

C 6%   (C)

D 8%   (D)

20 At a credit union in Trinidad, the interest rate on fixed deposits decreased from 8% per annum to 4% per annum due to the economic downturn. The difference in annual interest on a fixed deposit of $10 000 is

A $100   (A)

B $400   (B)

C $250   (C)

D $120   (D)

21 Five books are purchased at $80 each. All five are then sold for $300 altogether. What is the percentage loss?

A 10%   (A)

B 20%   (B)

C 25%   (C)

D 30%   (D)

22 Sam bought a video game for $800. Two days later he sold it for $1000. What is his profit as a percentage of cost price?

A 25%   (A)

B 20%   (B)

C 80%   (C)

D 10%   (D)

23 Adrian bought a bed at a discount of 20%, thus saving $200. What was the marked price of the bed?

A $800   Ⓐ

B $1200   Ⓑ

C $900   Ⓒ

D $1000   Ⓓ

24 A loan of $5000 was taken from the National Commercial Bank in June 2013. The loan was repaid in 2 years in equal monthly instalments of $300. What is the percentage profit on the loan?

A   22%   Ⓐ

B   44%   Ⓑ

C   20%   Ⓒ

D   18%   Ⓓ

Calculating commission

25 A store salesperson is paid 3% of his sales as a commission. He made sales of $2500. How much was his commission?

A $200   Ⓐ

B $75   Ⓑ

C $125   Ⓒ

D $50   Ⓓ

Calculating wages

26 Nathan is a plumber. He charges a fixed fee of $50 for a house visit and $20 per hour when he has to perform emergency repairs. Sydney calls Nathan to repair a flooded bathroom and he charges her $130. How many hours did Nathan spend fixing the problem?

A 1   (A)

B 2   (B)

C 3   (C)

D 4   (D)

27 The basic wage rate at Gibson Furniture store is $15 per hour. The overtime rate is one-and-a-half times the basic rate. A typical day's work is 8 hours. If Paul works for 10 hours his wage for that day is

A $120   (A)

B $45   (B)

C $165   (C)

D $150   (D)

4   Sets

Determining a given set using information provided

1 The set of factors of 12 is R. Therefore

A $R = \{\}$ (A)

B $R = \{1, 2, 3, 4, 6, 12\}$ (B)

C $R = \{1, 2, 3, 4\}$ (C)

D $R = \{1, 2, 3, 4, 6\}$ (D)

2 Which of the following sets is defined by $\{x \in Z : -4 \leq x \leq 3\}$?

A $\{1, 2, 3\}$ Ⓐ

B $\{0, 1, 2, 3\}$ Ⓑ

C $\{-4, -3, -2, -1, 0, 1, 2, 3\}$ Ⓒ

D $\{-3, -2, -1, 0, 1, 2\}$ Ⓓ

3 Which of the following sets is defined by $\{x \in Z : -2 \leq x < 4\}$?

A $\{0, 1, 2, 3\}$ Ⓐ

B $\{0, 1, 2, 3, 4\}$ Ⓑ

C $\{-1, 0, 1, 2, 3\}$ Ⓒ

D $\{-2, -1, 0, 1, 2, 3\}$ Ⓓ

4 Given that the set $P = \{\text{multiples of 4}\}$, which of the following could be set P?

A $\{1, 2, 4\}$ Ⓐ

B $\{4, 8, 12, 16\}$ Ⓑ

C $\{4, 18, 26\}$ Ⓒ

D $\{1, 2, 3, 4\}$ Ⓓ

Determining the number of subsets in a set

5 If $A = \{p, q, r\}$, then the number of subsets of A is

A 2   Ⓐ

B 6   Ⓑ

C 8   Ⓒ

D 3   Ⓓ

Understanding the meaning of an equivalent set

6 Which of the following sets is equivalent to {2, 4, 6, 8}?

A {2} (A)

B {2, 4} (B)

C {p, q, r} (C)

D {a, b, c, d} (D)

Understanding the meaning of the term subset

7 If A = {factors of 24} and B = {factors of 12}, then which of the following statements must be true?

A $A \subset B$ (A)

B $B \subset A$ (B)

C $A \cup B = \phi$ (C)

D $A \cap B = A$ (D)

8 In the Venn diagram below, which of the following are true about the sets A, B and C?

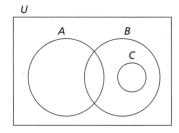

     I. $A \cap C = \varnothing$ II. $B \subset C$ III. $C \subset B$

A I only (A)

B I and II only (B)

C I and III only (C)

D II and III only (D)

Solving problems involving intersection and union of sets

9 If $A = \{1, 2, 3, 4\}$, $B = \{3, 4, 8\}$ and $C = \{3, 7, 9\}$, then $A \cap B \cap C =$

  A $\{\}$ Ⓐ

  B $\{3\}$ Ⓑ

  C $\{1, 2, 3, 4, 7, 8, 9\}$ Ⓒ

  D $\{3, 4\}$ Ⓓ

10 In a class of 35 students, 25 study chemistry and 22 study physics. What is the least number of students who are studying both chemistry and physics?

  A 6   Ⓐ

  B 8   Ⓑ

  C 9   Ⓒ

  D 12   Ⓓ

Solving problems involving the complement of a set

11 If $U = \{2, 4, 6, 8, 10\}$ and $P = \{4, 10\}$, then the number of elements in P' is

  A 2   Ⓐ

  B 3   Ⓑ

  C 4   Ⓒ

  D 5   Ⓓ

Shading Venn diagrams

12 In the Venn diagram below, what does the shaded area represent?

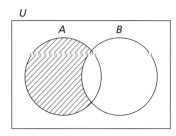

A A' Ⓐ

B B' Ⓑ

C $A \cap B'$ Ⓒ

D $A' \cap B$ Ⓓ

13 Which of the following diagrams represents $P \cap Q'$?

A    **C**

Ⓐ

Ⓑ

Ⓒ

B 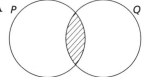   **D**

Ⓓ

14 Which of the following diagrams represents P'?

A 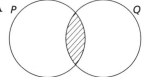   **C**

Ⓐ

Ⓑ

Ⓒ

B    **D**

Ⓓ

Understanding the meaning of a member of a set

15 p is a member of the set R. This statement can be written as

    A $p \in R$ Ⓐ

    B $p = \{\}$ Ⓑ

    C $p \cap R$ Ⓒ

    D $p \cup R$ Ⓓ

Understanding the concept of finite and infinite sets

16 Which of the following is an infinite set?

    A $P = \{$whole numbers between 5 and 12$\}$ Ⓐ

    B $Q = \{2, 4, 6, 8, 10\}$ Ⓑ

    C $R = \{$natural numbers less than 10$\}$ Ⓒ

    D $S = \{$multiples of 5$\}$ Ⓓ

Determining the number of elements in a given set

17 S and T are two finite sets. Given that

    $n(S) = 10$ $n(T) = 12$ $n(S \cap T) = 4$

    What is $n(S \cup T)$?

    A 18   Ⓐ

    B 6   Ⓑ

    C 8   Ⓒ

    D 20   Ⓓ

18 In the Venn diagram below, $n(A) = 7$, $n(B) = 13$ and $n(A \cup B) = 16$.

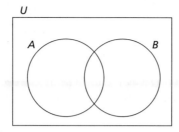

What is $n(A \cap B)$?

A 4   Ⓐ

B 9   Ⓑ

C 3   Ⓒ

D 8   Ⓓ

19 If $A = \{2, 3, 5, 8, 13\}$, then $n(A) =$

A 2   Ⓐ

B 4   Ⓑ

C 5   Ⓒ

D 6   Ⓓ

20 Given that $A = \{1, 4, 7, 9, 12\}$ and $B = \{3, 6, 7, 9, 13\}$, what is $n(A \cap B)$?

A 1   Ⓐ

B 7   Ⓑ

C 9   Ⓒ

D 2   Ⓓ

Determining information provided in a Venn diagram

21 If P = {multiples of 2 less than 14} and Q = {factors of 24}, then in the diagram below the shaded region represents

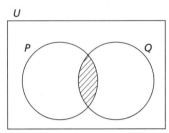

A {2, 4, 6}   Ⓐ

B {2, 4, 6, 8, 12}   Ⓑ

C {2, 4, 6, 12}   Ⓒ

D {2, 4}   Ⓓ

Items 22–24 are based on the Venn diagram below.

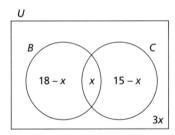

The diagram illustrates the members of a sports club who play basketball (B) and cricket (C).

There are 37 members in the sports club.

22 How many members play both basketball and cricket?

A 2   Ⓐ

B 3   Ⓑ

C 4   Ⓒ

D 5   Ⓓ

23 How many members play cricket only?

A 15   (A)

B 13   (B)

C 2   (C)

D 18   (D)

24 How many members play neither cricket nor basketball?

A 0   (A)

B 2   (B)

C 18   (C)

D 6   (D)

Items 25–27 are based on the information below.

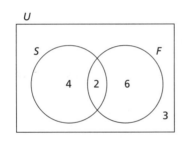

S = {students studying Spanish}

F = {students studying French}

25 How many students study Spanish?

A 4   (A)

B 6   (B)

C 3   (C)

D 2   (D)

26 How many students study neither Spanish nor French?

A 4   Ⓐ

B 2   Ⓑ

C 6   Ⓒ

D 3   Ⓓ

27 How many students study French only?

A 2   Ⓐ

B 4   Ⓑ

C 6   Ⓒ

D 3   Ⓓ

28 The Venn diagram below shows information relating to students studying accounts, maths and physics.

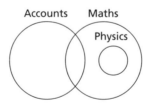

Which of the following statements can be made, based on the information provided?

I.   All students who study physics study maths.

II.   Some students who study accounts study physics.

III. Some students who study maths study accounts.

A I only   Ⓐ

B I and II only   Ⓑ

C I and III only   Ⓒ

D I, II and III   Ⓓ

Items 29 and 30 are based on the Venn diagram below.

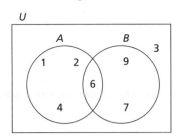

29 $n(A) =$

A $\{1, 2, 4, 6\}$ Ⓐ

B 4   Ⓑ

C 6   Ⓒ

D 2   Ⓓ

30 $(A \cup B)' =$

A $\{6\}$ Ⓐ

B $\{1, 2, 4, 6, 7, 9\}$ Ⓑ

C $\{3\}$ Ⓒ

D $\{1, 2, 3, 4, 6, 7, 9\}$ Ⓓ

5   Measurement

Calculating the perimeter of shapes

1 The lengths of the sides of a triangle are x cm, $2x$ cm and $3x$ cm. The perimeter of the triangle is 24 cm. What is the value of x?

A 3   Ⓐ

B 4   Ⓑ

C 5   Ⓒ

D 6   Ⓓ

2 The lengths of the sides of a triangle are $(x - 1)$ cm, $(x + 3)$ cm and $(x + 6)$ cm. The perimeter of the triangle is 26 cm. What is the length of the longest side?

A 5 cm   Ⓐ

B 9 cm   Ⓑ

C 10 cm   Ⓒ

D 12 cm   Ⓓ

3 What is the perimeter of the following shape?

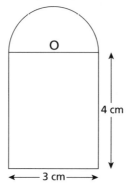

A $11 + \dfrac{3\pi}{2}$ cm   Ⓐ

B $11 + 3\pi$ cm   Ⓑ

C $7 + \dfrac{3\pi}{2}$ cm   Ⓒ

D $7 + 3\pi$ cm   Ⓓ

4 The perimeter of a square is 24 cm. What is the area of the square?

A 24 cm^2 Ⓐ

B 36 cm^2 Ⓑ

C 40 cm^2 Ⓒ

D 32 cm^2 Ⓓ

Calculating the area of shapes

5 The area of a rectangle is 48 cm². The length is halved and the breadth is tripled. What is the new area, in cm²?

A 24 cm²   Ⓐ

B 36 cm²   Ⓑ

C 72 cm²   Ⓒ

D 108 cm²   Ⓓ

6 The area of a triangle is 36 cm² and the length of its base is 8 cm. What is the perpendicular height, in cm, of the triangle?

A 4.5 cm   Ⓐ

B 18 cm   Ⓑ

C 6 cm   Ⓒ

D 9 cm   Ⓓ

7 The diagram below shows two concentric circles with centre O. The inner circle has a radius of 6 cm and the outer circle has a radius of 8 cm.

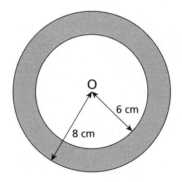

What is the area of the shaded region?

A 64π   Ⓐ

B 36π   Ⓑ

C 28π   Ⓒ

D 28π²   Ⓓ

8 What is the area of the figure below?

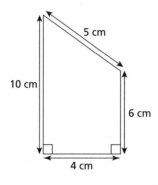

A 32 cm^2

B 40 cm^2

C 25 cm^2

D 48 cm^2

Ⓐ

Ⓑ

Ⓒ

Ⓓ

9 What is the area of the parallelogram shown below?

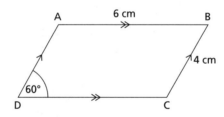

A $6 \times 4 \times \sin 60°$ cm^2

B $6 \times 4 \times \cos 60°$ cm^2

C $6 \times 4 \times \tan 60°$ cm^2

D 6×4 cm^2

Ⓐ

Ⓑ

Ⓒ

Ⓓ

10 What is the area of the following shape?

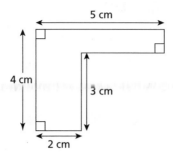

A 10 cm^2 Ⓐ

B 12 cm^2 Ⓑ

C 11 cm^2 Ⓒ

D 17 cm^2 Ⓓ

Calculating the surface area

11 The total surface area of a cube is 54 cm^2. What is the length of one side of the cube?

A 9 cm   Ⓐ

B 3 cm   Ⓑ

C 12 cm   Ⓒ

D 6 cm   Ⓓ

Calculating volume

12 The volume of a cube with an edge 5 cm long is

A 25 cm^3 Ⓐ

B 125 cm^3 Ⓑ

C 225 cm^3 Ⓒ

D 10 cm^3 Ⓓ

13 The diagram below shows a cylinder. The radius of the circular section is 2 cm and the length of the cylinder is 10 cm. What is the volume of the cylinder?

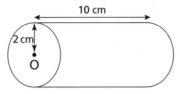

A 20π cm^2 Ⓐ

B 25π cm^2 Ⓑ

C 30π cm^2 Ⓒ

D 40π cm^2 Ⓓ

Calculating the circumference of a circle

14 The circumference of a circle is 44 cm. What is the radius of the circle?

A 22π Ⓐ

B $\dfrac{22}{\pi}$ Ⓑ

C $\dfrac{44}{\pi}$ Ⓒ

D $22\pi^2$ Ⓓ

15 The diagram below shows a sector of a circle with centre O. The length of the minor arc AB is 6 cm.

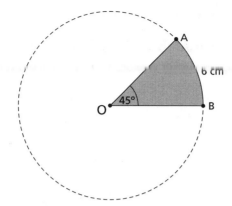

What is the circumference of the circle?

A 12 cm Ⓐ

B 36 cm Ⓑ

C 60 cm Ⓒ

D 48 cm Ⓓ

16 The circumference of a circle is 176 cm. Using $\pi = \dfrac{22}{7}$, what is the diameter of the circle?

A 28 cm Ⓐ

B 56 cm Ⓑ

C 88 cm Ⓒ

D 44 cm Ⓓ

Calculating the perimeter and the area of a sector

17 A sector AOB is such that angle AOB = 30° and OA = OB = 5 cm. What is the area of the sector?

A $\dfrac{30}{360} \times \pi \times 5^2$ Ⓐ

B $\dfrac{1}{12} \times \pi \times 5$ Ⓑ

C $\dfrac{30}{360} \times \pi^2 \times 5^2$ Ⓒ

D $\dfrac{1}{6} \times \pi \times 5^2$ Ⓓ

18 OAB is a sector of a circle with AOB = 60° and OA = 7 cm.

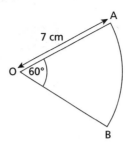

What is the length of the arc AB? Use $\pi = \dfrac{22}{7}$.

A $\dfrac{22}{6}$ cm   (A)

B $\dfrac{11}{6}$ cm   (B)

C $\dfrac{11}{3}$ cm   (C)

D $\dfrac{22}{3}$ cm   (D)

19 OAB is a sector of a circle with AOB = 30° and OA = 12 cm.

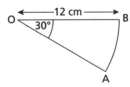

What is the area of the sector AOB?

A 18π cm^2 (A)

B 12π cm^2 (B)

C 32π cm^2 (C)

D 16π cm^2 (D)

20 The diagram below shows a circle with centre O and radius of 10 cm. AB is a chord of length 16 cm.

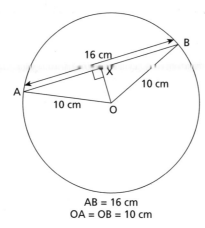

AB = 16 cm
OA = OB = 10 cm

What is the length OX?

A 4 cm

B 5 cm

C 6 cm

D 8 cm

(A)

(B)

(C)

(D)

Calculating the area of a trapezium

21 Which of the following shapes has an area exactly equal to $\frac{1}{2}(2+5) \times 7$ cm^2?

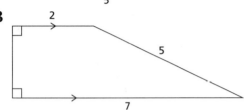

A

2

$\frac{7}{2}$

5

Ⓐ

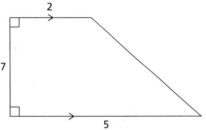

B

2

5

7

Ⓑ

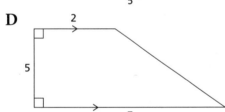

C

2

7

5

Ⓒ

D

2

5

7

Ⓓ

22 What is the area of the trapezium below?

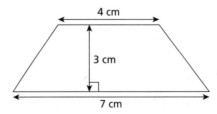

4 cm

3 cm

7 cm

A 16.5 cm^2 Ⓐ

B 84 cm^2 Ⓑ

C 24.5 cm^2 Ⓒ

D 14 cm^2 Ⓓ

Converting units

23 How many kilograms are there in 2.5 tonnes?

A 250   (A)

B 2500   (B)

C 25 000   (C)

D 250 000   (D)

24 A water dispenser contains 8 litres of water when full. A cup holds 250 cm^3 of water. How many cups of water can be obtained from the water dispenser?

A 16   (A)

B 32   (B)

C 25   (C)

D 18   (D)

25 Patrick drinks several bottles of soft drinks each day. Each bottle has a capacity of 200 ml. On a particular day he drinks 4 bottles of soft drinks. How many litres did he drink?

A 0.5 litres   (A)

B 0.8 litres   (B)

C 8 litres   (C)

D 0.08 litres   (D)

Calculating speed and distance in a given time interval

26 A car leaves a gas station at 06:20 hours and travels at a constant speed of 60 km h^{-1}. The car arrives at a breakfast shed at 7:05 hours. Assuming that the car did not stop along the way, the distance travelled is

A 45 km   (A)

B 40 km   (B)

C 80 km   (C)

D 75 km   (D)

27 Shawn works the night shift at a security company. He leaves home at 23:45 hours and reaches work at 01:10 hours. How long did he take to arrive at work?

A 1 hour 15 min   (A)

B 1 hour 20 min   (B)

C 1 hour 25 min   (C)

D 1 hour 10 min   (D)

Finding the distance when given a scale on a map

28 The distance between two towns is 20 km. When measured on a map, the distance between the two towns is 8 cm. The scale on the map is

A 1 : 25 000   (A)

B 1 : 250 000   (B)

C 1 : 20 000   (C)

D 1 : 200 000   (D)

Calculating the size of exterior angles in a polygon

29 The size of each exterior angle of a regular polygon is 60°. How many sides does the polygon have?

A 4   (A)

B 5   (B)

C 6   (C)

D 8   (D)

Estimating the mode, median and mean using data provided

Items 1–3 refer to the table below.

Kashav throws a six-sided die several times and records the number (score) obtained each time. The table below shows his results.

Number	1	2	3	4	5	6
Frequency	4	6	3	5	2	5

1 The modal score is

A 2   Ⓐ

B 3   Ⓑ

C 4   Ⓒ

D 6   Ⓓ

2 The median score is

A 3   Ⓐ

B 4   Ⓑ

C 5   Ⓒ

D 6   Ⓓ

3 The mean score is

A 3.4   Ⓐ

B 4.2   Ⓑ

C 5   Ⓒ

D 5.7   Ⓓ

4 The table below shows the frequency distribution of the lengths of pieces of wood in a pile, to the nearest centimetre.

Length, x (cm)	Frequency, f	xf
4	3	12
5	6	30
6	4	24
7	a	b
8	2	16
Total		96

How many times did a length of 7 cm occur?

A 2   Ⓐ

B 4   Ⓑ

C 6   Ⓒ

D 8   Ⓓ

5 If the mean of five numbers 2, 5, 8, x and 14 is 7, then x is

A 6   Ⓐ

B 35   Ⓑ

C 7   Ⓒ

D 5   Ⓓ

6 What is the median of the following numbers?

6, 5, 9, 5, 4, 3, 1, 8, 4, 4

A 4   Ⓐ

B 4.5   Ⓑ

C 5   Ⓒ

D 5.5   Ⓓ

7 The mean of a list of 6 numbers is 8. If the number 15 is added to the list, the new mean is

    A 6   (A)

    B 7   (B)

    C 8   (C)

    D 9   (D)

Items 8–12 relate to the set of scores obtained by six students in a quiz.

Students' scores: 3, 6, 10, 8, 6, 9

8 The median score is

    A 6   (A)

    B 7   (B)

    C 8   (C)

    D 9   (D)

9 The modal score is

    A 6   (A)

    B 7   (B)

    C 8   (C)

    D 9   (D)

10 The range of the scores is

    A 6   (A)

    B 7   (B)

    C 8   (C)

    D 9   (D)

11 The interquartile range of the scores is

A 1   (A)

B 2   (B)

C 3   (C)

D 4   (D)

12 The mean score is

A 6   (A)

B 6.5   (B)

C 7   (C)

D 7.5   (D)

13 The mean of 25 scores is 60. If each score is increased by 2, what is the new mean?

A 61   (A)

B 62   (B)

C 64   (C)

D 50   (D)

14 The mean of 10 numbers is 18. If the numbers 7 and 9 are removed, what is the new mean?

A 20.5   (A)

B 22   (B)

C 19   (C)

D 25   (D)

Interpreting a pie chart

15 100 children are asked to name their favourite flavour of a particular milk drink. The information is represented on the pie chart below.

Estimate the number of children who chose vanilla as their favourite flavour.

A 20   Ⓐ

B 25   Ⓑ

C 50   Ⓒ

D 80   Ⓓ

16 Daniel spends 30% of his salary on rent, 20% on food, 10% on transportation and the remainder goes into savings. On a pie chart, what is the angle of the sector representing savings?

A 108°   Ⓐ

B 216°   Ⓑ

C 120°   Ⓒ

D 144°   Ⓓ

17 The pie chart below shows the various modes of transportation used by a group of people to travel within their country.

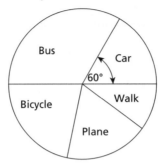

If 24 people use a bus, then the total number of people in the group is

A 72   Ⓐ

B 144   Ⓑ

C 100   Ⓒ

D 48   Ⓓ

Interpreting a bar chart

18 A bag is filled with differently coloured marbles. The bar chart below illustrates the distribution of the colours present in the bag.

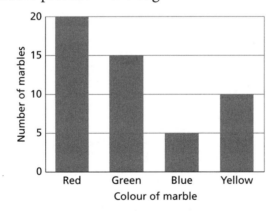

How many marbles are there in the bag?

A 15   Ⓐ

B 20   Ⓑ

C 40   Ⓒ

D 50   Ⓓ

Determining class boundaries given class intervals

19 The heights of people in a room were measured, to the nearest centimetre. The information is grouped and shown in the table below.

Height (cm)	160 164	165 169	170 174	175 179
Frequency	6	15	8	3

The class boundaries are

A 160, 164, 165, 169, 170, 174, 175, 179   Ⓐ

B 159.5, 164.5, 169.5, 174.5, 179.5   Ⓑ

C 6, 15, 8, 3   Ⓒ

D 4, 4, 4, 4   Ⓓ

Estimating the range of a given set of data

20 The table below shows the ages of the people in an auditorium.

Age	22	25	27	30	33	35	36	39
Number of people	2	5	7	10	12	6	2	1

The range of the ages is

A 44   Ⓐ

B 17   Ⓑ

C 12   Ⓒ

D 2   Ⓓ

Interpreting a cumulative frequency curve

Items 21–24 refer to the data below.

The diagram below illustrates the cumulative frequency curve for data collected after an examination was taken.

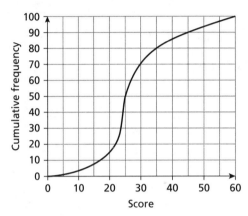

21 An estimate of the median score is

    A 50   Ⓐ

    B 21   Ⓑ

    C 25   Ⓒ

    D 60   Ⓓ

22 An estimate of the lower quartile is

    A 20   Ⓐ

    B 23   Ⓑ

    C 25   Ⓒ

    D 32   Ⓓ

23 An estimate of the upper quartile is

A 20   Ⓐ

B 23   Ⓑ

C 75   Ⓒ

D 32   Ⓓ

24 An estimate of the semi-interquartile range is

A 4.5   Ⓐ

B 9   Ⓑ

C 30   Ⓒ

D 50   Ⓓ

Calculating probabilities

25 A bag contains 3 blue, 5 red and 7 green balls. The probability of drawing a red ball from the bag at random is

A $\dfrac{3}{15}$ Ⓐ

B $\dfrac{1}{5}$ Ⓑ

C $\dfrac{1}{3}$ Ⓒ

D $\dfrac{2}{5}$ Ⓓ

26 12 000 students sat the CSEC Maths examination. The probability of a randomly selected student passing the examination is $\dfrac{3}{5}$. How many students failed the examination?

A 7200   Ⓐ

B 4800   Ⓑ

C 5000   Ⓒ

D 3200   Ⓓ

27 All the letters of the word EXAMINATION are written individually on identical pieces of paper. The pieces of paper are placed in a bowl and a random selection is made. What is the probability of drawing a letter 'N'?

A $\frac{1}{11}$ Ⓐ

B $\frac{1}{5}$ Ⓑ

C $\frac{2}{5}$ Ⓒ

D $\frac{2}{11}$ Ⓓ

28 There are 35 students in a form 5 CSEC Maths class. There are 15 boys in the class. What is the probability that a student chosen at random is a girl?

A $\frac{15}{35}$ Ⓐ

B $\frac{3}{7}$ Ⓑ

C $\frac{4}{7}$ Ⓒ

D $\frac{25}{35}$ Ⓓ

29 The table below shows the heights of seedlings in a tray (to the nearest centimetre).

Height (cm)	10	11	12	13	14	15	16	17	18
Number of seedlings	1	1	2	6	10	12	8	7	3

What is the probability that a seedling chosen at random has a height less than 14 cm?

A $\frac{2}{5}$ Ⓐ

B $\frac{1}{5}$ Ⓑ

C $\frac{1}{25}$ Ⓒ

D $\frac{10}{25}$ Ⓓ

30 A die is thrown twice. What is the probability of getting a five followed by an odd number?

A $\dfrac{1}{6} \times \dfrac{1}{6}$ Ⓐ

B $\dfrac{1}{6} \times \dfrac{3}{5}$ Ⓑ

C $\dfrac{1}{6} \times \dfrac{1}{2}$ Ⓒ

D $\dfrac{1}{6} \times \dfrac{2}{6}$ Ⓓ

31 A bowl contains 3 red marbles, 4 blue marbles and 3 green marbles. What is the probability of randomly selecting a marble that is not green?

A $\dfrac{3}{10}$ Ⓐ

B $\dfrac{4}{10}$ Ⓑ

C $\dfrac{7}{10}$ Ⓒ

D $\dfrac{1}{10}$ Ⓓ

7   Algebra

Simplifying and removing brackets

1 $-3(x - 2) =$

A $-3x - 2$ Ⓐ

B $-3x - 6$ Ⓑ

C $3x + 6$ Ⓒ

D $-3x + 6$ Ⓓ

2 $2x(x + 3y) - y(2x - 4y) =$

A $2x^2 + 6xy + 4y^2$ Ⓐ

B $2x^2 + 4xy + 4y^2$ Ⓑ

C $2x^2 + 2xy - 4y^2$ Ⓒ

D $2x^2 - 4xy + 4y^2$ Ⓓ

3 $\dfrac{27x - 18}{3} =$

   A $9x$ (A)

   B $6x - 9$ (B)

   C $9x - 6$ (C)

   D $9x + 6$ (D)

4   If $a = 5(p - q)$, then $10p$ is equal to

   A $2(a + 5q)$ (A)

   B $2(a + 2q)$ (B)

   C $a + 5q$ (C)

   D $a + 2q$ (D)

5 $2x(2 + 3y) - 3x(1 - 2y) =$

   A $x + 12xy$ (A)

   B $5x$ (B)

   C $-x$ (C)

   D $5x - 12xy$ (D)

Using binary operators

6   Given that $x \star y = 2x^2 - y$, then $(-2) \star 1 =$

   A 7 (A)

   B 8 (B)

   C -9 (C)

   D -2 (D)

7 If $a \star b = \dfrac{\sqrt{ab - b}}{a^2}$, then $3 \star 2 =$

   A $\dfrac{2}{9}$ Ⓐ

   B $\dfrac{9}{2}$ Ⓑ

   C $\dfrac{3}{4}$ Ⓒ

   D 4 Ⓓ

Simplifying using rules of indices

8 $3(ab^2)^3 =$

   A $3a^4b^6$ Ⓐ

   B $3a^3b^6$ Ⓑ

   C $9ab$ Ⓒ

   D $27a^3b^5$ Ⓓ

9 The expression $(3x)^3$ is equivalent to

   A $9x$ Ⓐ

   B $27x^3$ Ⓑ

   C $9x^3$ Ⓒ

   D $27x$ Ⓓ

10 $(-3pq^2)(-2p^3q) =$

   A $6p^4q^3$ Ⓐ

   B $-6p^4q^3$ Ⓑ

   C $5p^4q^3$ Ⓒ

   D $5p^3q^2$ Ⓓ

11 $3^8 \div 3^{-2} =$

  A 3^6 Ⓐ

  B 3^{10} Ⓑ

  C $\dfrac{1}{3^6}$ Ⓒ

  D $\dfrac{1}{3^{10}}$ Ⓓ

Solving linear equations

12 Given that $6(x - 2) - 3(x - 1) = 6$, the value of x is

  A 4   Ⓐ

  B 5   Ⓑ

  C 6   Ⓒ

  D 7   Ⓓ

13 If $\dfrac{3x}{100} = 27$, then $x =$

  A 0.9   Ⓐ

  B 9   Ⓑ

  C 90   Ⓒ

  D 900   Ⓓ

14 If $3x - 25 = x + 17$, then $x =$

  A 10   Ⓐ

  B 15   Ⓑ

  C 18   Ⓒ

  D 21   Ⓓ

15 If $(2x - 1) - 6(x - 1) + 7 = 0$, then $x =$

A 1   Ⓐ

B 2   Ⓑ

C 3   Ⓒ

D 4   Ⓓ

Solving linear inequalities

16 If x is an integer that satisfies the inequalities $12 < x - 3 < 24$, then the smallest possible value of x is

A 12   Ⓐ

B 13   Ⓑ

C 15   Ⓒ

D 16   Ⓓ

17 Given that $3x - 2 \leq 13$, the range of values of x is

A $x \leq 5$ Ⓐ

B $x \leq 15$ Ⓑ

C $x \geq 5$ Ⓒ

D $x \geq 5$ Ⓓ

18 Given $125 < 5 - 3x$, the range of values of x is

A $x > 40$ Ⓐ

B $x < 20$ Ⓑ

C $x > -20$ Ⓒ

D $x < -40$ Ⓓ

Solving worded problems using algebra

19 Amaria has x books in her school bag. Arya has three times as many books in her bag. Arya removes two books from her bag. In terms of x, how many books does she now have in her bag?

   A $x - 2$ Ⓐ

   B $3(x - 2)$ Ⓑ

   C $3x + 2$ Ⓒ

   D $3x - 2$ Ⓓ

20 The length and width of a rectangle are $(x + 2)$ cm and 4 cm, respectively. The perimeter of the rectangle is $8x$. Which of the following equations can be used to solve for x?

   A $2(x + 2) + 4 = 8x$ Ⓐ

   B $2(x + 2 + 4) = 8x$ Ⓑ

   C $x + 2 + 4 = 8x$ Ⓒ

   D $4(x + 2) = 8x$ Ⓓ

21 Currently, Nyla's age is six times the age of her daughter Anya. Two years ago Nyla's age was $(2x - 4)$. What is Anya's present age?

   A $\dfrac{x - 1}{3}$ Ⓐ

   B $\dfrac{2x - 4}{6}$ Ⓑ

   C $\dfrac{2x - 1}{6}$ Ⓒ

   D $6(2x - 4) + 2$ Ⓓ

22 The sum of three consecutive positive integers is 24. The smallest integer is $x - 1$. Which of the following expresses the information given?

   A $x + 1 + x + 2 + x + 3 = 24$ Ⓐ

   B $3x + 1 = 24$ Ⓑ

   C $x - 1 + x + x + 1 = 24$ Ⓒ

   D $x - 1 + 2(x - 1) + 3(x - 1) = 24$ Ⓓ

23 When 7 is subtracted from a certain number and the result is multiplied by 2 the final number is 18. What is the original number?

A 16   (A)

B 9   (B)

C 14   (C)

D 11   (D)

24 Which of the following represents the statement 'Two times the difference of two square numbers is negative'?

A $2x^2 - y^2 < 0$ (A)

B $2(x - y) < 0$ (B)

C $2(x^2 - y^2) < 0$ (C)

D $2(x^2 - y^2) > 0$ (D)

25 The perimeter of a triangle is 12 cm. If the lengths of the sides are x cm, $(x - 1)$ cm and $(x - 2)$ cm, then the length of the longest side is

A 3 cm   (A)

B 4 cm   (B)

C 5 cm   (C)

D 6 cm   (D)

26 When 5 is added to 4 times a certain number x, the result is 19. This statement can be represented by

A $4x + 5 = 19$ (A)

B $5x + 4 = 19$ (B)

C $4x + 19 = 5$ (C)

D $5x + 4 = 14$ (D)

27 The angles in a triangle are x, $\frac{1}{2}x$ and $3x$. What is the size of the largest angle?

A 20° Ⓐ

B 40° Ⓑ

C 120° Ⓒ

D 30° Ⓓ

Simplifying algebraic fractions

28 $\dfrac{5x}{3y} + \dfrac{2x}{5y}$ may be written as

A $\dfrac{7x}{8y}$ Ⓐ

B $\dfrac{31x}{15y}$ Ⓑ

C $\dfrac{31x}{15y^2}$ Ⓒ

D $\dfrac{7x}{15y}$ Ⓓ

29 $\dfrac{2a}{5b} - \dfrac{7c}{2d} =$

A $-\dfrac{5ac}{3bd}$ Ⓐ

B $\dfrac{4ad - 35bc}{10bd}$ Ⓑ

C $\dfrac{14ac}{10bd}$ Ⓒ

D $\dfrac{35bc - 4ad}{10bd}$ Ⓓ

Solving problems involving direct and indirect variation

30 Given that y varies inversely as the square of x, if k is the constant of proportionality, then

A $y = kx$ Ⓐ

B $y = kx^2$ Ⓑ

C $y = \dfrac{k}{x^2}$ Ⓒ

D $y = \dfrac{k}{\sqrt{x}}$ Ⓓ

31 y is inversely proportional to the square of x. When $x = 2$, $y = 9$. When $x = 3$,

A $y = 4$ Ⓐ

B $y = 6$ Ⓑ

C $y = 12$ Ⓒ

D $y = 24$ Ⓓ

32 y is directly proportional to x. When $x = -3$, $y = 15$. Therefore, when $x = 2$, $y =$

A -5 Ⓐ

B -10 Ⓑ

C 5 Ⓒ

D 10 Ⓓ

Substituting constants into algebraic expressions

33 If $x = -2$ and $y = 3$. Then $yx =$

A $-\dfrac{2}{3}$ Ⓐ

B $\dfrac{1}{9}$ Ⓑ

C -9 Ⓒ

D -6 Ⓓ

34 If $p = 2$ and $pq = 8$, then $(p + q)^2 - p^2 - q^2 =$

A 10   (A)

B 16   (B)

C 32   (C)

D 18   (D)

35 $R = \dfrac{2a^2}{1-b}$. When $a = -2$ and $b = -3$, $R =$

A 6   (A)

B 8   (B)

C 3   (C)

D 2   (D)

Changing the subject of the formula

36 If $y = k\sqrt{\dfrac{x}{m}}$, then

A $m = x\sqrt{\dfrac{y}{k}}$ (A)

B $m = \dfrac{k^2 x}{y^2}$ (B)

C $m = \dfrac{y^2}{k^2 x}$ (C)

D $m = \dfrac{kx^2}{y}$ (D)

Factorising expressions

37 $9 - 4x^2 =$

   A $(3 - 2x)(3 - 2x)$ Ⓐ

   B $(9 - 4x)(9 + 4x)$ Ⓑ

   C $9(3 - 4x)$ Ⓒ

   D $(3 - 2x)(3 + 2x)$ Ⓓ

38 $2x^2 - x - 3 =$

   A $(x - 1)(2x + 3)$ Ⓐ

   B $(x + 1)(2x - 3)$ Ⓑ

   C $(2x + 1)(2x - 1)$ Ⓒ

   D $(2x + 3)(2x - 3)$ Ⓓ

Solving simultaneous equations

39 What are the solutions to the pair of simultaneous equations below?

$x + 3y = 33$

$3x - 2y = 0$

   A $x = 9$ and $y = 6$ Ⓐ

   B $x = 6$ and $y = 9$ Ⓑ

   C $x = 3$ and $y = 4$ Ⓒ

   D $x = 9$ and $y = -6$ Ⓓ

40 Given that

$2x + 3y = 3$

$3x - 6y = 15$

Which of the following pairs of x and y satisfies both equations?

   A $x = 3, y = 1$ Ⓐ

   B $x = 3, y = -1$ Ⓑ

   C $x = -2, y = 1$ Ⓒ

   D $x = 2, y = -1$ Ⓓ

Finding the midpoint, gradient and equation of a straight line

1 The equation of a line is given by $1 - 2y = 6x$. The gradient of the line is

    A 6   Ⓐ

    B −6   Ⓑ

    C 3   Ⓒ

    D −3   Ⓓ

2 The coordinates of points A and B are (2, 8) and (−2, −4), respectively. The gradient of the line AB is

    A 3   Ⓐ

    B −3   Ⓑ

    C $\dfrac{1}{3}$ Ⓒ

    D $-\dfrac{1}{3}$ Ⓓ

3 The coordinates of points P and Q are (2, 8) and (−2, −4), respectively. The coordinates of the midpoint of the line PQ are

    A (2, 6)   Ⓐ

    B (0, 2)   Ⓑ

    C (−2, 6)   Ⓒ

    D (2, 0)   Ⓓ

4 Which of the following represents the equation of a straight line?

    A $2 = x + 3y$ Ⓐ

    B $y = \dfrac{2}{x}$ Ⓑ

    C $y = 2x^2 + 3x + 1$ Ⓒ

    D $y = x^3$ Ⓓ

5 The equation of the line which passes through the point $(0, -3)$ and has a gradient of $\frac{1}{2}$ is

A $y = -3x + \frac{1}{2}$ Ⓐ

B $y = \frac{1}{2}x + 3$ Ⓑ

C $y = \frac{1}{2}x - 3$ Ⓒ

D $y = 2x + 3$ Ⓓ

6 Which of the following points lies on the line $y = 3x + 2$?

A $(2, 7)$ Ⓐ

B $(-1, -1)$ Ⓑ

C $(0, 3)$ Ⓒ

D $(3, 10)$ Ⓓ

Identifying parallel and perpendicular lines

7 The gradient of the line P is 2. Which of the following lines is parallel to P?

A $y = 3x + 2$ Ⓐ

B $2y = 2x - 5$ Ⓑ

C $3y = 6x + 2$ Ⓒ

D $4 - 2x = y$ Ⓓ

8 A line R has the equation $2y = 3 - x$. Which of the following lines is perpendicular to R?

A $y = 2x + 1$ Ⓐ

B $y = -2x + 3$ Ⓑ

C $x = 2y - 4$ Ⓒ

D $6y = x + 1$ Ⓓ

Items 9–11 are based on the diagram below.

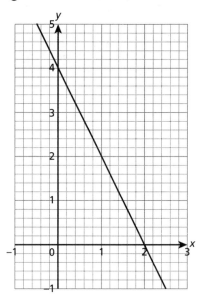

9 What is the gradient of the line?

A $\frac{1}{2}$ Ⓐ

B 2   Ⓑ

C –2   Ⓒ

D $-\frac{1}{2}$ Ⓓ

10 The straight line cuts the *y*-axis at

A (0, 2)   Ⓐ

B (2, 0)   Ⓑ

C (4, 0)   Ⓒ

D (0, 4)   Ⓓ

11 What is the equation of the straight line?

A $y = 2x - 4$ Ⓐ

B $y = 4 - \dfrac{1}{2}x$ Ⓑ

C $y = 4 - 2x$ Ⓒ

D $y = 2x + 4$ Ⓓ

Interpreting quadratic functions

Items 12–14 are based on the graph below.

The graph below shows the curve $y = x^2 + 2x - 3$.

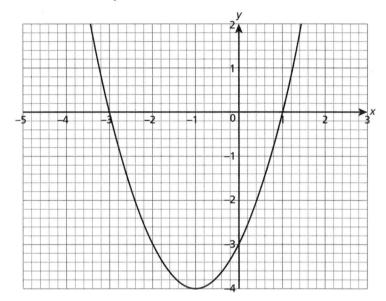

12 The values of x for which $y = x^2 + 2x - 3$ intersects $y = 0$ are

A $x = -3$ and $x = 1$ Ⓐ

B $x = -1$ and $x = -3$ Ⓑ

C $x = -3$ and $x = -4$ Ⓒ

D $x = -3$ and $x = 2$ Ⓓ

13 The minimum point of $y = x^2 + 2x - 3$ is

A $(-3, 0)$ Ⓐ

B $(0, -3)$ Ⓑ

C $(-1, -4)$ Ⓒ

D $(1, 0)$ Ⓓ

14 From the graph, the values of x when $y = -3$ are

A $x = -3$ and $x = 1$ Ⓐ

B $x = -2$ and $x = 0$ Ⓑ

C $x = -2.5$ and $x = 1$ Ⓒ

D $x = -2.2$ and $x = 0.2$ Ⓓ

15 The diagram below shows the graph of the function $y = -x^2 + 6x - 8$.

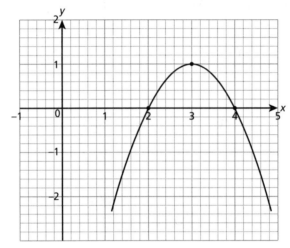

The values of x for which $y = -x^2 + 6x - 8$ intersects $y = 0$ are

A $x = 2$ and $x = 1$ Ⓐ

B $x = 0$ and $x = 1$ Ⓑ

C $x = 0$ and $x = 4$ Ⓒ

D $x = 2$ and $x = 4$ Ⓓ

Items 16–19 are based on the diagram below.

The graph below represents the function $f(x)$.

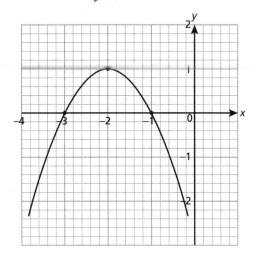

16 Which of the following expressions represents the function $f(x)$?

   A $-x^2 + 4x - 3$ Ⓐ

   B $x^2 + 4x + 3$ Ⓑ

   C $x^2 + 4x - 3$ Ⓒ

   D $-x^2 - 4x - 3$ Ⓓ

17 What is the axis of symmetry of the graph?

   A $x = -2$ Ⓐ

   B $x = -1$ Ⓑ

   C $x = -3$ Ⓒ

   D $x = 0$ Ⓓ

18 The maximum value of $f(x)$ is

   A -2 Ⓐ

   B -1 Ⓑ

   C 1 Ⓒ

   D 2 Ⓓ

19 The range of values for which $f(x) > 0$ is

A $x > -1$ and $x < -3$ Ⓐ

B $-3 < x < -1$ Ⓑ

C $x > 0$ Ⓒ

D $x < 0$ Ⓓ

20 The graph below shows the function $f(x)$.

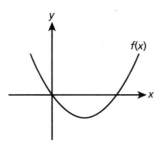

Which of the following could be an expression for $f(x)$?

A $x - 3x^2$ Ⓐ

B $2x^2 - x$ Ⓑ

C $4x^2 + x$ Ⓒ

D $x - 2x^2$ Ⓓ

21 A quadratic function is defined by $f(x) = x^2 - 3x - 10$. What is the axis of symmetry when this quadratic function is plotted?

A $x = -3$ Ⓐ

B $x = \dfrac{-3}{2}$ Ⓑ

C $x = \dfrac{3}{2}$ Ⓒ

D $x = -10$ Ⓓ

22 Which of the following quadratic functions has a maximum value?

A $f(x) = x^2 + 3x + 7$ Ⓐ

B $f(x) = 7 + 2x - 5x^2$ Ⓑ

C $f(x) - 3x^2 - 6x$ Ⓒ

D $f(x) = 2x^2$ Ⓓ

23 The graph below shows the function $f(x) = x^2 - 3x - 3$.

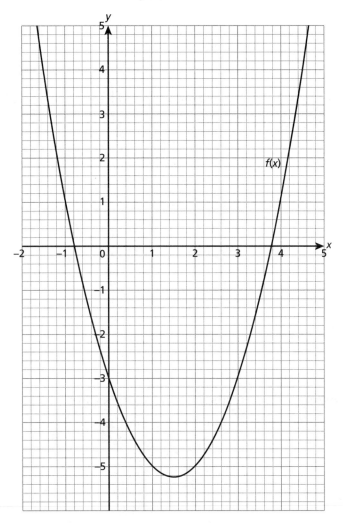

The interval domain for which $f(x) < 1$ is

A $x > 4, x < -1$ Ⓐ

B $-1 < x < 4$ Ⓑ

C $x > 3.75, x < -0.75$ Ⓒ

D $x > 1.5$ Ⓓ

Completing the square

24 Given that $3x^2 + 6x - 2 = a(x + h)^2 + k$, what are the values of a, h and k?

A $a = 3$, $h = 1$ and $k = -5$ Ⓐ

B $a = 3$, $h = -1$ and $k = -2$ Ⓑ

C $a = 3$, $h = 3$ and $k = -5$ Ⓒ

D $a = 3$, $h = 1$ and $k = 5$ Ⓓ

25 Given that $y = 2x^2 - 5x + 3$ can be written as $y = 2\left(x - \dfrac{5}{4}\right)^2 - \dfrac{1}{8}$. The coordinates of the minimum point are

A $\left(\dfrac{5}{4}, \dfrac{1}{8}\right)$ Ⓐ

B $\left(\dfrac{-5}{4}, \dfrac{-1}{8}\right)$ Ⓑ

C $\left(\dfrac{5}{4}, \dfrac{-1}{8}\right)$ Ⓒ

D $\left(\dfrac{10}{4}, \dfrac{-1}{8}\right)$ Ⓓ

Relations

26 Which of the following best describes the relation below?

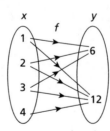

A x is less than y Ⓐ

B x is greater than y Ⓑ

C x is a factor of y Ⓒ

D x is a multiple of y Ⓓ

27 Which of the following best describes the relation below?

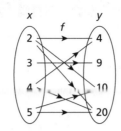

A x is a multiple of y Ⓐ

B x is greater than y Ⓑ

C x is a factor of y Ⓒ

D x is less than y Ⓓ

Identifying a function

28 Which of the following does NOT represent a function?

A
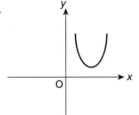

C
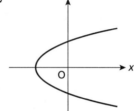

Ⓐ

Ⓑ

Ⓒ

Ⓓ

B
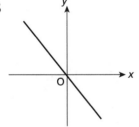

D
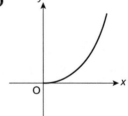

29 Which of the following represents a function?

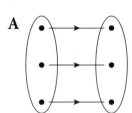

Ⓐ
Ⓑ
Ⓒ
Ⓓ

Functions

30 If $f(x) = 3x^2 - 2$, then $f(-2) =$

A 10

B −14

C 34

D −6

Ⓐ
Ⓑ
Ⓒ
Ⓓ

31 Which of the following sets is represented by the function $f: x \to 2x^2 + 1$, where $x \in \{0, 1, 2, 3\}$?

A $\{(0, 1), (1, 3), (2, 5), (3, 7)\}$

B $\{(0, 1), (1, 3), (2, 9), (3, 19)\}$

C $\{(0, 1), (1, 2), (2, 3), (3, 4)\}$

D $\{(0, 1), (1, 6), (2, 12), (3, 18)\}$

Ⓐ
Ⓑ
Ⓒ
Ⓓ

32 If $g(x) = \dfrac{4x - 5}{2}$, then $g(-5) =$

A 12   Ⓐ

B 12.5   Ⓑ

C −12.5   Ⓒ

D 6   Ⓓ

33 Which of the following best describes the function below?

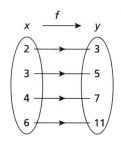

A $f(x) = 2x - 1$ Ⓐ

B $f(x) = 2(x - 1)$ Ⓑ

C $y = f(x)$ Ⓒ

D $x = f(2x - 1)$ Ⓓ

34 Which function describes the following?

$\{(0, -1), (1, 1), (2, 3), (3, 5)\}$

A $y = 2x + 1$ Ⓐ

B $y = 2x - 1$ Ⓑ

C $y = 3x - 1$ Ⓒ

D $y = 3x + 1$ Ⓓ

Determining a composite function

Items 35–38 are based on the functions below.

$$f(x) = 6x - 4$$
$$g(x) = \frac{3x - 7}{2}$$

35 $f(-2) =$

   A −12   Ⓐ

   B −16   Ⓑ

   C 16   Ⓒ

   D 8   Ⓓ

36 $g(5) =$

   A 4   Ⓐ

   B 5   Ⓑ

   C 6   Ⓒ

   D 7   Ⓓ

37 $fg(x) =$

   A $9x + 25$ Ⓐ

   B $3x + 18$ Ⓑ

   C $9x - 21$ Ⓒ

   D $9x - 25$ Ⓓ

38 gf(x) =

   A $\dfrac{18x - 19}{2}$ Ⓐ

   B $\dfrac{18x - 11}{2}$ Ⓑ

   C $\dfrac{18x + 19}{2}$ Ⓒ

   D $\dfrac{18x - 25}{2}$ Ⓓ

Items 39–43 are based on the following functions.

   $f(x) = 2x + 3$

   $g(x) = x^2 - 2$

39 f(−3) =

   A −9   Ⓐ

   B −3   Ⓑ

   C 9   Ⓒ

   D 3   Ⓓ

40 $f^{-1}(x)$ =

   A $\dfrac{x - 3}{2}$ Ⓐ

   B $\dfrac{x + 3}{2}$ Ⓑ

   C $2x - 3$ Ⓒ

   D $\dfrac{x}{2} - 3$ Ⓓ

41 $f^{-1}(-1) =$

    A 2   Ⓐ

    B −2   Ⓑ

    C 5   Ⓒ

    D 3   Ⓓ

42 $fg(2) =$

    A 7   Ⓐ

    B 30   Ⓑ

    C 21   Ⓒ

    D 47   Ⓓ

43 $(fg)^{-1}(x) =$

    A $\dfrac{x+1}{2}$ Ⓐ

    B $\sqrt{\dfrac{x-1}{2}}$ Ⓑ

    C $\sqrt{\dfrac{x+1}{2}}$ Ⓒ

    D $\dfrac{x+3}{2}$ Ⓓ

Finding the inverse of a function

44 $f(x) = 3x - 2$. Therefore, $f^{-1}(x) =$

    A $3x + 2$ Ⓐ

    B $2 - 3x$ Ⓑ

    C $\dfrac{x-2}{3}$ Ⓒ

    D $\dfrac{x+2}{3}$ Ⓓ

Representing an inequality graphically and on a number line

45 The number line below represents which of the following inequalities?

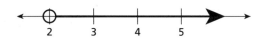

- **A** $x \geq 2$
- **B** $x > 2$
- **C** $x \leq 2$
- **D** $x < 2$

(A)
(B)
(C)
(D)

46 The number line below is defined by which of the following inequalities?

- **A** $-1 \leq x \leq 3$
- **B** $-1 < x < 3$
- **C** $-1 \geq x > 3$
- **D** $-1 \geq x \geq 3$

(A)
(B)
(C)
(D)

47 Which of the following represents the inequality $4 \leq x < 7$?

A

4 5 6 7

B

4 5 6 7

C

4 5 6 7

D

4 5 6 7

(A)
(B)
(C)
(D)

48 Which of the following inequalities describes the shaded region in the diagram below?

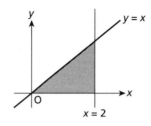

A $y \leq 0, y \leq x, x \geq 2$ (A)

B $y \geq 0, y \leq x, x \geq 2$ (B)

C $y \geq 0, y \geq x, x \leq 2$ (C)

D $y \geq 0, y \leq x, x \leq 2$ (D)

49 In the graph below, the shaded region can be represented by

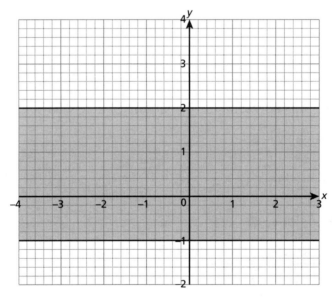

A $\{(x, y): -4 \leq y \leq 3\}$ (A)

B $\{(x, y): 0 \leq y \leq 2\}$ (B)

C $\{(x, y): -1 \leq y \leq 0\}$ (C)

D $\{(x, y): -1 \leq y \leq 2\}$ (D)

Solving problems using linear programming

50 A farmer in Jamaica wants to buy some cows and sheep. The land that he owns is capable of supporting 50 animals. He intends to purchase at least one of each animal. One cow costs $ 1200 and one sheep costs $ 600. The farmer can spend no more than $ 15 000. If c and s are used to represent the number of cows and sheep, respectively, which of the following inequalities can be used to represent all the information provided?

A $c \geq 1, s \geq 1, c + s \leq 50, 1200c + 600s \leq 15\,000$ (A)

B $c \leq 1, s \leq 1, c + s \geq 50, 1200c + 600s \geq 15\,000$ (B)

C $c \geq 1, s \geq 1, c + s \leq 50, 1200c + 600s \geq 15\,000$ (C)

D $c \geq 1, s \geq 1, c + s \leq 50, 12c + 6s \geq 150$ (D)

Items 51 and 52 are based on the information given below.

A company manufactures two brands of dish-washing liquid, brand x and brand y. The company has a warehouse that can store a maximum of 500 bottles of dish-washing liquid. On a daily basis, the company must produce at least 80 bottles of brand x and no more than 250 bottles of brand y. When sold, the profit made on brand x is $8 and the profit made on brand y is $12.

51 Which of the following inequalities represent the information provided?

A $x \leq 80, y \geq 250, x + y \leq 500$ (A)

B $x \geq 80, y \leq 250, x + y \geq 500$ (B)

C $x \geq 80, y \geq 250, x + y \leq 500$ (C)

D $x \geq 80, y \leq 250, x + y \leq 500$ (D)

52 Which of the following equations can be used to determine the maximum profit made by selling brand x and brand y?

   A Maximum profit $= 8x + 12y$ Ⓐ

   B Maximum profit $= 80x + 250y$ Ⓑ

   C Maximum profit $= 12x + 8y$ Ⓒ

   D Maximum profit $= 2x + 3y$ Ⓓ

Items 53 and 54 are based on the information provided below.

A company manufactures two types of computer chips, brand A and brand B. For each unit of brand A sold, a profit of $500 is made. For each unit of brand B sold, a profit of $600 is made. When the computer chips are being manufactured, the following conditions must be satisfied.

Condition 1: $x \geq 0$

Condition 2: $y \geq 0$

Condition 3: $x \leq 5$

Condition 4: _____

The graph below shows the shaded region that satisfies all four conditions.

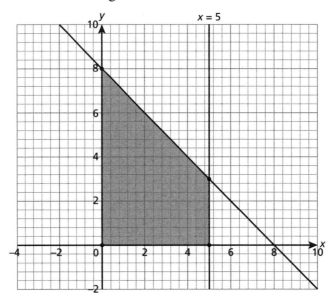

53 Based on the graph provided, what is condition 4?

A $x + y \geq 8$ (A)

B $x - y \leq 8$ (B)

C $x + y \leq 8$ (C)

D $x - y \geq 8$ (D)

54 What is the maximum profit that can be obtained by selling the two types of computer chips?

A $4300   (A)

B $4800   (B)

C $2500   (C)

D $5000   (D)

55 What can be said about the x and y coordinates of the point P in the diagram below?

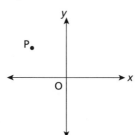

A x is positive and y is positive   (A)

B x is negative and y is positive   (B)

C x is positive and y is negative   (C)

D x is negative and y is negative   (D)

Finding the magnitude of an angle using construction lines

1 The diagram below shows the construction of the angle CAB. With the centre at A an arc BC is drawn. With the centre at B and the same radius, an arc PQ is drawn. With the centre at D and the same radius, an arc RS is drawn.

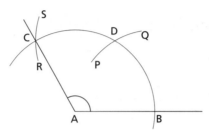

What size is the angle CAB?

A 90°   Ⓐ

B 60°   Ⓑ

C 120°   Ⓒ

D 110°   Ⓓ

Performing calculations involving trigonometric ratios (sine, cosine and tangent)

2 In the right-angled triangle below, $\cos \theta =$

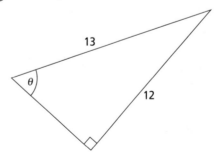

A $\dfrac{5}{12}$ Ⓐ

B $\dfrac{5}{13}$ Ⓑ

C $\dfrac{12}{13}$ Ⓒ

D $\dfrac{13}{12}$ Ⓓ

3 In the triangle below, tan $\theta =$

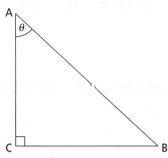

A $\dfrac{AC}{CB}$ Ⓐ

B $\dfrac{CB}{AB}$ Ⓑ

C $\dfrac{CB}{AC}$ Ⓒ

D $\dfrac{AB}{AC}$ Ⓓ

4 In the diagram below, $\sin(180° - \theta) =$

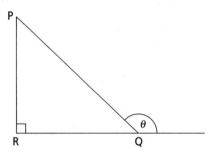

A $\dfrac{PR}{RQ}$ Ⓐ

B $\dfrac{PR}{PQ}$ Ⓑ

C $\dfrac{RQ}{PQ}$ Ⓒ

D $\dfrac{PQ}{PR}$ Ⓓ

5 In the diagram below what is the length of BC?

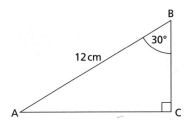

A 12 sin 30° Ⓐ

B 12 tan 30° Ⓑ

C 12 cos 30° Ⓒ

D 12 cos 60° Ⓓ

6 In the diagram below what is cos CAB?

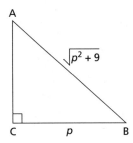

A $\dfrac{p}{\sqrt{p^2 + 9}}$ Ⓐ

B $\dfrac{3}{p}$ Ⓑ

C $\dfrac{\sqrt{p^2 + 9}}{3}$ Ⓒ

D $\dfrac{3}{\sqrt{p^2 + 9}}$ Ⓓ

7 In the diagram below, which trigonometric ratio is equal to $\frac{3}{5}$?

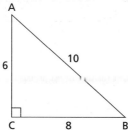

A sin A   Ⓐ

B cos A   Ⓑ

C tan B   Ⓒ

D cos B   Ⓓ

Items 8–11 are based on the diagram below.

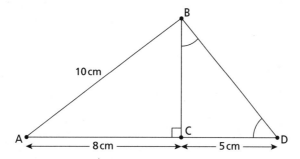

8 What is the length of BC?

A 4 cm   Ⓐ

B 6 cm   Ⓑ

C 9 cm   Ⓒ

D 7 cm   Ⓓ

9 tan CDB =

A $\dfrac{6}{5}$ Ⓐ

B $\dfrac{5}{6}$ Ⓑ

C $\dfrac{5}{8}$ Ⓒ

D $\dfrac{8}{5}$ Ⓓ

10 cos CBD =

A $\dfrac{5}{\sqrt{61}}$ Ⓐ

B $\dfrac{6}{\sqrt{61}}$ Ⓑ

C $\dfrac{5}{6}$ Ⓒ

D $\dfrac{6}{5}$ Ⓓ

11 Angle CDB =

A $\sin^{-1}\left(\dfrac{5}{6}\right)$ Ⓐ

B $\cos^{-1}\left(\dfrac{5}{6}\right)$ Ⓑ

C $\tan^{-1}\left(\dfrac{6}{5}\right)$ Ⓒ

D $\tan^{-1}\left(\dfrac{5}{6}\right)$ Ⓓ

Performing calculations involving parallel lines and triangles

12 In the diagram below lines PQ and RS are parallel.

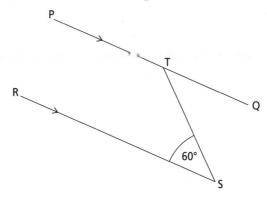

What is the angle STQ?

A 120°   (A)

B 60°   (B)

C 30°   (C)

D 20°   (D)

13 Lines AB and CD intersect as shown below.

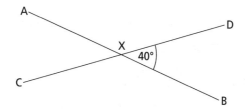

Angle AXD is

A 40°   (A)

B 50°   (B)

C 120°   (C)

D 140°   (D)

14 The diagram below shows two parallel lines PQ and RS. BAC = 45° and QBC = 60°.

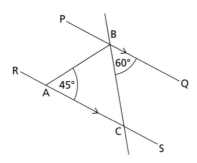

What is the size of angle ABC?

A 60° Ⓐ

B 40° Ⓑ

C 95° Ⓒ

D 75° Ⓓ

Items 15 and 16 are based on the diagram below.

The diagram shows two parallel lines AB and CD. The line PQ intersects AB and CD at Y and X, respectively. Angle QYB = 52°.

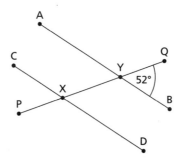

15 Angle PXD =

A 52° Ⓐ

B 120° Ⓑ

C 128° Ⓒ

D 108° Ⓓ

16 Angle CXP =

A 52°　　　　　　　　　　　　　　　　　　　　　　Ⓐ

B 120°　　　　　　　　　　　　　　　　　　　　　Ⓑ

C 128°　　　　　　　　　　　　　　　　　　　　　Ⓒ

D 108°　　　　　　　　　　　　　　　　　　　　　Ⓓ

17 In the diagram below, angle AOD =

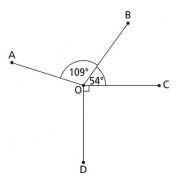

A 100°　　　　　　　　　　　　　　　　　　　　　Ⓐ

B 107°　　　　　　　　　　　　　　　　　　　　　Ⓑ

C 120°　　　　　　　　　　　　　　　　　　　　　Ⓒ

D 110°　　　　　　　　　　　　　　　　　　　　　Ⓓ

18 The diagram below shows two parallel lines AB and CD. The line EF intersects CD at the point G.

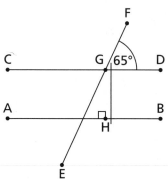

Angle EGH =

A 65°　　　　　　　　　　　　　　　　　　　　　　Ⓐ

B 35°　　　　　　　　　　　　　　　　　　　　　　Ⓑ

C 25°　　　　　　　　　　　　　　　　　　　　　　Ⓒ

D 45°　　　　　　　　　　　　　　　　　　　　　　Ⓓ

19 In the diagram below, what is the size of angle CAB?

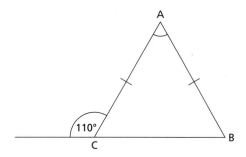

A 40° Ⓐ

B 70° Ⓑ

C 30° Ⓒ

D 45° Ⓓ

20 In the triangle below, AB = BC. What is the size of angle ABC?

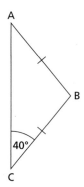

A 140° Ⓐ

B 120° Ⓑ

C 100° Ⓒ

D 110° Ⓓ

21 In the diagram below, the length AC can be found using the equation:

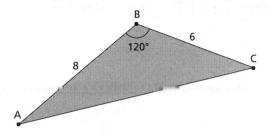

A $AC^2 = 8^2 + 6^2 - (2 \times 8 \times 6 \times \cos 120°)$ Ⓐ

B $AC^2 = 8^2 + 6^2 + (2 \times 8 \times 6 \times \cos 120°)$ Ⓑ

C $AC^2 = 8^2 + 6^2 - (2 \times 8 \times 6 \times \cos 60°)$ Ⓒ

D $AC^2 = 8^2 + 6^2 - (2 \times 8 \times 6 \times \sin 120°)$ Ⓓ

Performing calculations involving circle geometry

22 In the diagram below, angle PRQ is

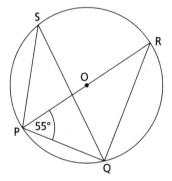

A 35°   Ⓐ

B 90°   Ⓑ

C 25°   Ⓒ

D 30°   Ⓓ

23 In the diagram below, θ =

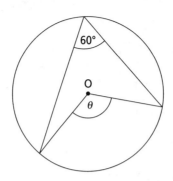

A 30° (A)

B 60° (B)

C 100° (C)

D 120° (D)

24 In the diagram below, O is the centre of the circle. LM = LN and angle MON = 100°.

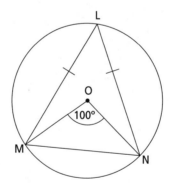

Angle OML =

A 25° (A)

B 50° (B)

C 35° (C)

D 20° (D)

25 In the diagram below, angle AOC =

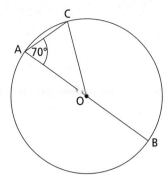

A 70°   (A)

B 110°   (B)

C 40°   (C)

D 30°   (D)

26 In the diagram below, angle ABC =

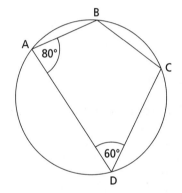

A 100°   (A)

B 120°   (B)

C 60°   (C)

D 80°   (D)

27 The diagram below shows a cyclic quadrilateral.

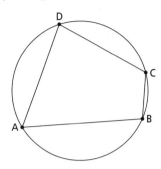

Which of the following statements is true?

A A + B = 180°

B A + C = 180°

C A + D = 180°

D A + C = 90°

Ⓐ

Ⓑ

Ⓒ

Ⓓ

Items 28 and 29 refer to the diagram below.

The diagram below shows a quadrilateral BCDE inscribed inside a circle of centre O.

Angle DBA = 63°

Angle CBE = 57°

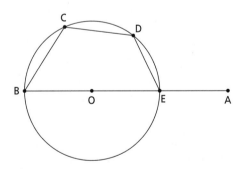

28 What is the magnitude of angle DEA?

A 117°

B 123°

C 120°

D 45°

Ⓐ

Ⓑ

Ⓒ

29 What is the magnitude of angle BCD?

    A 117°   Ⓐ

    B 57° Ⓑ

    C 120° Ⓒ

    D 63° Ⓓ

Items 30–32 are based on the information below.

The diagram below shows a circle with centre O. The line PQ is a tangent to the circle at the point A.

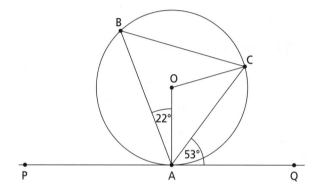

30 What is the magnitude of angle ABC?

    A 127° Ⓐ

    B 75° Ⓑ

    C 53° Ⓒ

    D 62° Ⓓ

31 What is the magnitude of angle AOC?

    A 106° Ⓐ

    B 112° Ⓑ

    C 53° Ⓒ

    D 100° Ⓓ

32 What is the magnitude of angle BAP?

   A 48°   Ⓐ

   B 75°   Ⓑ

   C 53°   Ⓒ

   D 68°   Ⓓ

Identifying types of triangles

33 A triangle with all its sides equal is called a(n)

   A Scalene triangle   Ⓐ

   B Isosceles triangle   Ⓑ

   C Right-angled triangle   Ⓒ

   D Equilateral triangle   Ⓓ

34 A triangle with two equal sides is called a(n)

   A Scalene triangle   Ⓐ

   B Isosceles triangle   Ⓑ

   C Right-angled triangle   Ⓒ

   D Equilateral triangle   Ⓓ

35 A triangle that has one angle that is 90° is called a(n)

   A Scalene triangle   Ⓐ

   B Isosceles triangle   Ⓑ

   C Right-angled triangle   Ⓒ

   D Equilateral triangle   Ⓓ

Performing calculations involving Pythagoras' theorem

36 What is the length of DC in the diagram below?

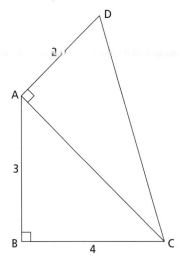

A 5   Ⓐ

B $\sqrt{7}$ Ⓑ

C $\sqrt{29}$ Ⓒ

D 8   Ⓓ

Performing calculations involving bearings

37 James and John are travelling in a small fishing boat on a bearing of 180° from the island of Barbados. What direction are they travelling in?

A North   Ⓐ

B South   Ⓑ

C West   Ⓒ

D East   Ⓓ

38 A ship is travelling on a bearing of 135°. In what direction is the ship travelling?

A South-east   Ⓐ

B North-east   Ⓑ

C South-west   Ⓒ

D South   Ⓓ

39 The diagram below shows two points P and Q. North lines are represented by the letter N. The bearing of Q from P is represented by which angle?

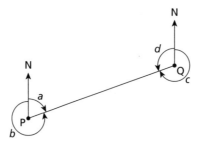

A a   Ⓐ

B b   Ⓑ

C c   Ⓒ

D d   Ⓓ

Items 40–42 are based on the information below.

The diagram shows the position of three ships A, B and C relative to each other in the Caribbean Sea. The North line is drawn at each of the positions.

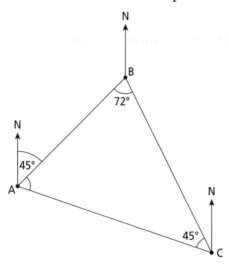

40 What is the bearing of B from A?

   A 045°   Ⓐ

   B 072°   Ⓑ

   C 117°   Ⓒ

   D 135°   Ⓓ

41 What is the bearing of C from B?

   A 135°   Ⓐ

   B 45°   Ⓑ

   C 120°   Ⓒ

   D 153°   Ⓓ

42 What is the bearing of A from C?

A 135°   Ⓐ

B 288°   Ⓑ

C 280°   Ⓒ

D 270°   Ⓓ

Identifying properties of shapes

43 Which of the following is NOT a quadrilateral?

A A hexagon   Ⓐ

B A square   Ⓑ

C A rhombus   Ⓒ

D A rectangle   Ⓓ

44 How many lines of symmetry does a square have?

A 1   Ⓐ

B 2   Ⓑ

C 4   Ⓒ

D 6   Ⓓ

45 What is the order of rotational symmetry for a rectangle?

A 0   Ⓐ

B 1   Ⓑ

C 2   Ⓒ

D 4   Ⓓ

Describing translations

46 In the diagram below, AB is translated to A′B′.

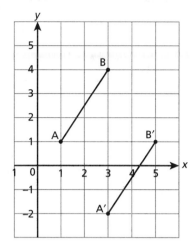

The vector that translates AB to A′B′ may be described as

A $\begin{pmatrix} 2 \\ -3 \end{pmatrix}$ **C** $\begin{pmatrix} 3 \\ -2 \end{pmatrix}$ Ⓐ

                                             Ⓑ

B $\begin{pmatrix} 2 \\ 3 \end{pmatrix}$ **D** $\begin{pmatrix} -3 \\ 2 \end{pmatrix}$ Ⓒ

                                             Ⓓ

47 The image of the point A (2, 3) after undergoing a translation **T** is A′ (5, 1). What is the translation vector?

A $\begin{pmatrix} 2 \\ -3 \end{pmatrix}$ Ⓐ

B $\begin{pmatrix} 2 \\ 3 \end{pmatrix}$ Ⓑ

C $\begin{pmatrix} 3 \\ 4 \end{pmatrix}$ Ⓒ

D $\begin{pmatrix} 3 \\ -2 \end{pmatrix}$ Ⓓ

Describing reflections

48 Which of the following shows a reflection in the line $y = 0$?

A 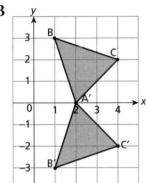 Ⓐ

B 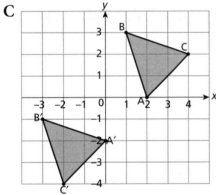 Ⓑ

C Ⓒ

D 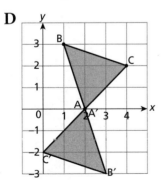 Ⓓ

49 The diagram below shows a point P.

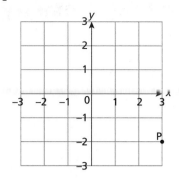

The point P is reflected in the *y*-axis. What are the coordinates of its image P′ after the reflection?

A (3, 2)   Ⓐ

B (−3, −2)   Ⓑ

C (2, 3)   Ⓒ

D (2, −3)   Ⓓ

50 The image of the point A (1, −3) when reflected in the line *y* = 2 is

A (7, 1)   Ⓐ

B (1, 7)   Ⓑ

C (1, 4)   Ⓒ

D (1, 6)   Ⓓ

Describing rotations

51 The graph below shows the line $y = 2x$.

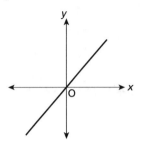

The line $y = 2x$ is rotated 45° in a clockwise direction about the origin O. Which of the following represents the image of this transformation?

A $y = -x$ Ⓐ

B $x = 0$ Ⓑ

C $y = 0$ Ⓒ

D $y = x$ Ⓓ

52 What type of transformation maps triangle ABC onto triangle A′B′C′?

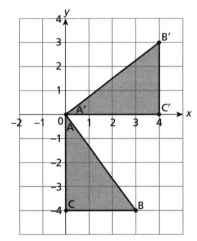

A An enlargement   Ⓐ

B A reflection   Ⓑ

C A translation   Ⓒ

D A rotation   Ⓓ

53 The point P (2, −4) undergoes a rotation of 90° in a clockwise direction about the point (0, 0). What are the coordinates of the image P′?

A (−4, −2)   Ⓐ

B (4, 2)   Ⓑ

C (−4, 2)   Ⓒ

D (2, 4)   Ⓓ

Describing enlargements

Items 54 and 55 are based on the information below.

In an enlargement, triangle ABC is mapped onto triangle A′B′C′. The centre of enlargement is the point (1, 0).

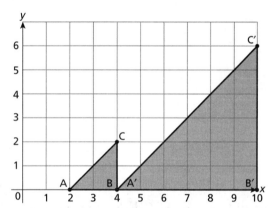

54 What is the scale factor of this enlargement?

A 2   Ⓐ

B 3   Ⓑ

C $\dfrac{1}{2}$ Ⓒ

D $\dfrac{1}{3}$ Ⓓ

55 The area of triangle ABC is a. What is the area of triangle A′B′C′?

A $6a$ Ⓐ

B $9a$ Ⓑ

C $3a$ Ⓒ

D $9a^2$ Ⓓ

56 Triangle ABC undergoes an enlargement to produce triangle A′B′C′. The object and image are congruent. Which of the following could be the value of the scale factor?

A 2   Ⓐ

B $\dfrac{1}{2}$ Ⓑ

C 1   Ⓒ

D −2   Ⓓ

57 Triangle ABC undergoes an enlargement of scale factor 2, to produce the image triangle A′B′C′. The area of triangle ABC is 6 square units. What is the area of triangle A′B′C′?

A 6 square units   Ⓐ

B 18 square units   Ⓑ

C 3 square units   Ⓒ

D 24 square units   Ⓓ

Recognising angles of depression and elevation

58 In the diagram below, the angle of depression of the point Q from point R is 60°.

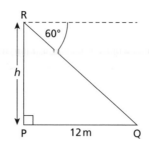

If PQ = 12 m, what is the height h?

A $12 \times \tan 60°$ (A)

B $12 \times \sin 60°$ (B)

C $12 \times \cos 60°$ (C)

D $\dfrac{12}{\tan 60°}$ (D)

59 In the diagram below, the angle of elevation of point A from point P is 35°. The point P is 2 m above the ground.

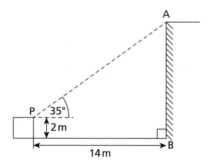

What is the distance AB?

A $2 + 14 \tan 35°$ (A)

B $2 + 14 \sin 35°$ (B)

C $2 + 14 \cos 35°$ (C)

D $14 \tan 35°$ (D)

Geometry and Trigonometry (cont.)

Similar triangles

60 In the diagram below, triangle ABC and triangle AED are similar.

BC = 10 cm   DE = 5 cm   AC = 12 cm

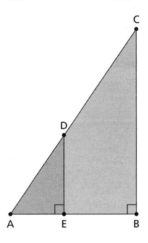

What is the length of AD?

A 8 cm   Ⓐ

B 4 cm   Ⓑ

C 6 cm   Ⓒ

D 4.5 cm   Ⓓ

10 Vectors and Matrices

Adding matrices

1 Given that $\mathbf{A} = \begin{pmatrix} 2 & 1 \\ 3 & 4 \end{pmatrix}$ and $\mathbf{B} = \begin{pmatrix} 1 & 2 \\ -1 & 3 \end{pmatrix}$, $\mathbf{A} + 2\mathbf{B} =$

A $\begin{pmatrix} 3 & 3 \\ 2 & 7 \end{pmatrix}$ **C** $\begin{pmatrix} 4 & 5 \\ 2 & 12 \end{pmatrix}$ Ⓐ

Ⓑ

B $\begin{pmatrix} 4 & 1 \\ 5 & 10 \end{pmatrix}$ **D** $\begin{pmatrix} 4 & 5 \\ 1 & 10 \end{pmatrix}$ Ⓒ

Ⓓ

2 If $A = \begin{pmatrix} 2 & 1 \\ 1 & -1 \end{pmatrix}$ and $B = \begin{pmatrix} 0 & 1 \\ -1 & 2 \end{pmatrix}$, then $A - 2B =$

A $\begin{pmatrix} 2 & -1 \\ 3 & 5 \end{pmatrix}$ 　　　　　C $\begin{pmatrix} 2 & -1 \\ 3 & -3 \end{pmatrix}$ 　Ⓐ

　　　　　　　　　　　　　　　　　　　　　　　Ⓑ

B $\begin{pmatrix} 2 & -1 \\ 1 & -5 \end{pmatrix}$ 　　　　　D $\begin{pmatrix} 2 & -1 \\ 3 & -4 \end{pmatrix}$ 　Ⓒ

　　　　　　　　　　　　　　　　　　　　　　　Ⓓ

Multiplying matrices

3 If $P = \begin{pmatrix} 1 & 3 \\ -1 & 2 \end{pmatrix}$ and $Q = \begin{pmatrix} 2 & -1 \\ -1 & 4 \end{pmatrix}$, then $PQ =$

A $\begin{pmatrix} -1 & 11 \\ -4 & 9 \end{pmatrix}$ 　　　　　C $\begin{pmatrix} 3 & 2 \\ 0 & 6 \end{pmatrix}$ 　Ⓐ

　　　　　　　　　　　　　　　　　　　　　　　Ⓑ

B $\begin{pmatrix} 2 & -3 \\ 1 & 8 \end{pmatrix}$ 　　　　　D $\begin{pmatrix} -2 & 12 \\ -3 & 8 \end{pmatrix}$ 　Ⓒ

　　　　　　　　　　　　　　　　　　　　　　　Ⓓ

4 If $P = \begin{pmatrix} 1 & 3 \\ -1 & 2 \end{pmatrix}$, then $P^2 =$

A $\begin{pmatrix} -2 & 9 \\ -3 & 1 \end{pmatrix}$ 　　　　　C $\begin{pmatrix} 1 & 3 \\ -1 & 2 \end{pmatrix}$ 　Ⓐ

　　　　　　　　　　　　　　　　　　　　　　　Ⓑ

B $\begin{pmatrix} 1 & 3 \\ -1 & 2 \end{pmatrix}$ 　　　　　D $\begin{pmatrix} 1 & 3 \\ -1 & 2 \end{pmatrix}$ 　Ⓒ

　　　　　　　　　　　　　　　　　　　　　　　Ⓓ

5 If $\begin{pmatrix} a & 1 \\ 1 & b \end{pmatrix}\begin{pmatrix} -1 & 1 \\ 2 & 0 \end{pmatrix} = \begin{pmatrix} 0 & 2 \\ 5 & 1 \end{pmatrix}$, then the value of a and of b are

A $a = 1$ and $b = 1$ Ⓐ

B $a = 2$ and $b = 3$ Ⓑ

C $a = 3$ and $b = 2$ Ⓒ

D $a = 2$ and $b = 4$ Ⓓ

Finding the determinant of a matrix

6 The determinant of the matrix $\mathbf{B} = \begin{pmatrix} 3 & 3 \\ -3 & 2 \end{pmatrix}$ is

A −15 Ⓐ

B 15 Ⓑ

C 3 Ⓒ

D −3 Ⓓ

Identifying and performing calculations involving singular matrices

7 Which of the following matrices is singular?

A $\begin{pmatrix} 2 & 3 \\ -1 & 2 \end{pmatrix}$ **C** $\begin{pmatrix} 2 & 4 \\ -1 & 2 \end{pmatrix}$ Ⓐ

Ⓑ

B $\begin{pmatrix} 3 & 6 \\ -2 & 4 \end{pmatrix}$ **D** $\begin{pmatrix} -2 & 4 \\ -1 & 2 \end{pmatrix}$ Ⓒ

Ⓓ

8 Given that $\mathbf{A} = \begin{pmatrix} 2p & 6 \\ -2 & 2 \end{pmatrix}$ is a singular matrix, what is the value of p?

A −3 Ⓐ

B 3 Ⓑ

C −4 Ⓒ

D 2 Ⓓ

Finding the inverse of a matrix

9 Which of the following is the identity matrix?

A $\begin{pmatrix} 0 & 1 \\ 1 & 0 \end{pmatrix}$

C $\begin{pmatrix} 1 & 0 \\ 0 & 1 \end{pmatrix}$

B $\begin{pmatrix} 0 & 1 \\ -1 & 0 \end{pmatrix}$

D $\begin{pmatrix} 1 & -1 \\ -1 & 1 \end{pmatrix}$

Ⓐ

Ⓓ

Ⓒ

Ⓓ

10 The inverse of the matrix $\mathbf{A} = \begin{pmatrix} 2 & 2 \\ -1 & 3 \end{pmatrix}$ is

A $\dfrac{1}{8}\begin{pmatrix} 2 & 2 \\ -1 & 3 \end{pmatrix}$

C $\dfrac{1}{4}\begin{pmatrix} 2 & 2 \\ -1 & 3 \end{pmatrix}$

B $\dfrac{1}{8}\begin{pmatrix} 3 & -2 \\ 1 & 2 \end{pmatrix}$

D $\dfrac{1}{4}\begin{pmatrix} 3 & -2 \\ 1 & 2 \end{pmatrix}$

Ⓐ

Ⓑ

Ⓒ

Ⓓ

Using a matrix method to solve a pair of simultaneous equations

11 Given that $\begin{pmatrix} 1 & 2 \\ 3 & -5 \end{pmatrix}\begin{pmatrix} x \\ y \end{pmatrix} = \begin{pmatrix} 4 \\ 1 \end{pmatrix}$ what are the values of x and y?

A $x = 1$ and $y = 2$

B $x = 2$ and $y = 1$

C $x = 3$ and $y = 2$

D $x = 2$ and $y = 3$

Ⓐ

Ⓑ

Ⓒ

Ⓓ

12 Yashoda uses the matrix method to solve the following pair of simultaneous equations.

$4x + y = 1$

$3x + 2y = 2$

In the last stage of her procedure she obtains the following

$$\begin{pmatrix} x \\ y \end{pmatrix} = \frac{1}{5} \begin{pmatrix} 2 & -1 \\ -3 & 4 \end{pmatrix} \begin{pmatrix} 1 \\ 2 \end{pmatrix}$$

What are the values of x and of y?

A $x = 0$ and $y = 2$ Ⓐ

B $x = 0$ and $y = 1$ Ⓑ

C $x = 1$ and $y = 0$ Ⓒ

D $x = 5$ and $y = 2$ Ⓓ

Using a matrix to represent a geometric transformation

13 The coordinates of point P are (–2, 3). What are the coordinates of the image P′ formed when P undergoes a translation of $\begin{pmatrix} -1 \\ 3 \end{pmatrix}$?

A (–3, 6)   Ⓐ

B (–2, 6)   Ⓑ

C (2, –3)   Ⓒ

D (6, –3)   Ⓓ

14 Which transformation matrix represents a reflection in the y-axis?

A $\begin{pmatrix} 1 & 0 \\ 0 & 1 \end{pmatrix}$ **C** $\begin{pmatrix} 0 & 1 \\ 1 & 0 \end{pmatrix}$ Ⓐ

   Ⓑ

B $\begin{pmatrix} -1 & 0 \\ 0 & 1 \end{pmatrix}$ **D** $\begin{pmatrix} 0 & -1 \\ -1 & 0 \end{pmatrix}$ Ⓒ

   Ⓓ

15 Which of the following transformation matrices represents a reflection in the line $y = x$?

A $\begin{pmatrix} 1 & 0 \\ 0 & -1 \end{pmatrix}$

C $\begin{pmatrix} 0 & 1 \\ 1 & 0 \end{pmatrix}$

B $\begin{pmatrix} -1 & 0 \\ 0 & 1 \end{pmatrix}$

D $\begin{pmatrix} 0 & -1 \\ -1 & 0 \end{pmatrix}$

(A)
(B)
(C)
(D)

16 The matrix $\begin{pmatrix} 3 & 0 \\ 0 & 3 \end{pmatrix}$ represents

A a reflection in the line $y = x$

(A)

B a rotation of 90° about the point (3, 3)

(B)

C an enlargement of scale of factor 3 about the origin O

(C)

D a reflection in the line $y = 3$

(D)

17 A point P (2, 1) undergoes a transformation M$\begin{pmatrix} 0 & -1 \\ 1 & 0 \end{pmatrix}$. What are the coordinates of P after the transformation?

A (−1, 2)

(A)

B (2, −1)

(B)

C (1, 1)

(C)

D (1, 2)

(D)

18 A point P (−2, −4) undergoes a transformation M$\begin{pmatrix} 0 & 1 \\ 1 & 0 \end{pmatrix}$. What are the coordinates of P after the transformation?

A (−4, 2)

(A)

B (4, −2)

(B)

C (2, 4)

(C)

D (−4, −2)

(D)

19 A transformation is performed on triangle ABC as follows:

A rotation of 90° in a clockwise direction about the origin, followed by a reflection in the y-axis.

The coordinates of A are (2, 1).

Which of the following can be used to determine A′, which is the final image of A after the combined transformation?

A $\begin{pmatrix} -1 & 0 \\ 0 & 1 \end{pmatrix}\begin{pmatrix} 0 & 1 \\ -1 & 0 \end{pmatrix}\begin{pmatrix} 2 \\ 1 \end{pmatrix}$

C $\begin{pmatrix} 0 & -1 \\ -1 & 0 \end{pmatrix}\begin{pmatrix} 0 & 1 \\ -1 & 0 \end{pmatrix}\begin{pmatrix} 2 \\ 1 \end{pmatrix}$

Ⓐ

Ⓑ

B $\begin{pmatrix} 0 & 1 \\ -1 & 0 \end{pmatrix}\begin{pmatrix} -1 & 0 \\ 0 & 1 \end{pmatrix}\begin{pmatrix} 2 \\ 1 \end{pmatrix}$

D $\begin{pmatrix} -1 & 0 \\ 0 & 1 \end{pmatrix}\begin{pmatrix} 0 & 1 \\ 1 & 0 \end{pmatrix}\begin{pmatrix} 2 \\ 1 \end{pmatrix}$

Ⓒ

Ⓓ

Finding the magnitude of a vector

20 The position vector of A relative to an origin O is $\begin{pmatrix} 3 \\ 4 \end{pmatrix}$. What is the magnitude of $\overrightarrow{OA}$?

A 25

Ⓐ

B 5

Ⓑ

C 7

Ⓒ

D 9

Ⓓ

21 Given that

$$\overrightarrow{OA} = \begin{pmatrix} 2 \\ 4 \end{pmatrix}$$

$$\overrightarrow{OB} = \begin{pmatrix} -1 \\ 2 \end{pmatrix}$$

Then $\overrightarrow{AB} =$

A $\begin{pmatrix} 1 \\ 2 \end{pmatrix}$ **C** $\begin{pmatrix} 3 \\ 2 \end{pmatrix}$ Ⓐ

Ⓑ

B $\begin{pmatrix} -1 \\ -2 \end{pmatrix}$ **D** $\begin{pmatrix} -3 \\ -2 \end{pmatrix}$ Ⓒ

Ⓓ

Recognising parallel vectors

22 Which of the following vectors is parallel to $\overrightarrow{AB} = \begin{pmatrix} 2 \\ 3 \end{pmatrix}$?

A $\begin{pmatrix} 1 \\ 3 \end{pmatrix}$ **C** $\begin{pmatrix} 3 \\ 4 \end{pmatrix}$ Ⓐ

Ⓑ

B $\begin{pmatrix} -4 \\ -6 \end{pmatrix}$ **D** $\begin{pmatrix} 6 \\ 4 \end{pmatrix}$ Ⓒ

Ⓓ

Adding and subtracting vectors

Items 23–27 are based on the diagram below.

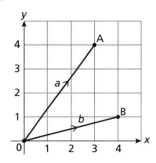

The diagram shows two position vectors $\overrightarrow{OA}$ and $\overrightarrow{OB}$

23 $\overrightarrow{OA}$ written as a column vector $\begin{pmatrix} x \\ y \end{pmatrix}$ is

A $\begin{pmatrix} 4 \\ 3 \end{pmatrix}$ C $\begin{pmatrix} 4 \\ 1 \end{pmatrix}$ Ⓐ

                                          Ⓑ

B $\begin{pmatrix} 3 \\ 4 \end{pmatrix}$ D $\begin{pmatrix} 1 \\ 4 \end{pmatrix}$ Ⓒ

                                          Ⓓ

24 $\overrightarrow{OB}$ written as a column vector $\begin{pmatrix} x \\ y \end{pmatrix}$ is

A $\begin{pmatrix} 4 \\ 3 \end{pmatrix}$ C $\begin{pmatrix} 4 \\ 1 \end{pmatrix}$ Ⓐ

                                          Ⓑ

B $\begin{pmatrix} 3 \\ 4 \end{pmatrix}$ D $\begin{pmatrix} 1 \\ 4 \end{pmatrix}$ Ⓒ

                                          Ⓓ

25 What is the magnitude of the vector $\overrightarrow{OA}$?

    A 3   Ⓐ

    B 4   Ⓑ

    C 5   Ⓒ

    D 2   Ⓓ

26 $\overrightarrow{AO}$ written as a column vector $\begin{pmatrix} x \\ y \end{pmatrix}$ is

    A $\begin{pmatrix} -4 \\ -3 \end{pmatrix}$ **C** $\begin{pmatrix} 4 \\ 1 \end{pmatrix}$ Ⓐ

                                                                                              Ⓑ

    B $\begin{pmatrix} -3 \\ -4 \end{pmatrix}$ **D** $\begin{pmatrix} 1 \\ 4 \end{pmatrix}$ Ⓒ

                                                                                               Ⓓ

27 $\overrightarrow{AB}$ written as a column vector $\begin{pmatrix} x \\ y \end{pmatrix}$ is

    A $\begin{pmatrix} 3 \\ -1 \end{pmatrix}$ **C** $\begin{pmatrix} 4 \\ 1 \end{pmatrix}$ Ⓐ

                                                                                              Ⓑ

    B $\begin{pmatrix} -3 \\ 4 \end{pmatrix}$ **D** $\begin{pmatrix} 1 \\ -3 \end{pmatrix}$ Ⓒ

                                                                                               Ⓓ

Items 28–32 are based on the diagram below.

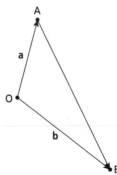

The diagram shows two vectors $\overrightarrow{OA} = \mathbf{a}$ and $\overrightarrow{OB} = \mathbf{b}$.

The vector $\mathbf{a}$ translates the point (2, 4) to the point (3, 6).

The vector $\mathbf{b}$ translates the point (−1, −3) to the point (4, −4).

28 Which of the following represents the vector $\overrightarrow{AB}$?

A $\mathbf{a} + \mathbf{b}$ Ⓐ

B $\mathbf{a} - \mathbf{b}$ Ⓑ

C $-\mathbf{a} + \mathbf{b}$ Ⓒ

D $\mathbf{a} - 2\mathbf{b}$ Ⓓ

29 $\mathbf{a}$ written as a column vector is

A $\begin{pmatrix} -1 \\ 2 \end{pmatrix}$ C $\begin{pmatrix} 2 \\ 1 \end{pmatrix}$ Ⓐ Ⓑ

B $\begin{pmatrix} 1 \\ 2 \end{pmatrix}$ D $\begin{pmatrix} -1 \\ -2 \end{pmatrix}$ Ⓒ Ⓓ

30 $\mathbf{b}$ written as a column vector is

A $\begin{pmatrix} -1 \\ 2 \end{pmatrix}$ C $\begin{pmatrix} 5 \\ 1 \end{pmatrix}$ Ⓐ Ⓑ

B $\begin{pmatrix} -5 \\ 1 \end{pmatrix}$ D $\begin{pmatrix} 5 \\ -1 \end{pmatrix}$ Ⓒ Ⓓ

31 The vector $\frac{1}{2}(\mathbf{a} + \mathbf{b}) =$

A $\begin{pmatrix} 6 \\ 1 \end{pmatrix}$ C $\begin{pmatrix} 0.5 \\ 3 \end{pmatrix}$ Ⓐ Ⓑ

B $\begin{pmatrix} 3 \\ 0.5 \end{pmatrix}$ D $\begin{pmatrix} -3 \\ 0.5 \end{pmatrix}$ Ⓒ Ⓓ

32 Which of the following vectors are parallel to $\mathbf{a} - 2\mathbf{b}$?

I. $\mathbf{a} + 2\mathbf{b}$

II. $2\mathbf{a} - 4\mathbf{b}$

III. $-6\mathbf{b} + 3\mathbf{a}$

A I only   Ⓐ

B I and III only   Ⓑ

C III only   Ⓒ

D II and III only   Ⓓ